Children
and Chess

CHILDREN AND CHESS

A Guide for Educators

Alexey W. Root

Foreword by Dr. John D. McNeil

Teacher Ideas Press, an imprint of Libraries Unlimited
Westport, Connecticut • London

Library of Congress Cataloging-in-Publication Data

Root, Alexey W.
  Children and chess : a guide for educators / by Alexey W. Root ;
foreword by Dr. John D. McNeil.
    p.   cm.
  Includes bibliographical references and index.
  ISBN 1-59158-358-6 (pbk. : alk. paper)
  1. Chess for children. 2. Chess—Study and teaching. I. Title.
  GV1446.R66   2006
  794.1'2—dc22   2006003878

British Library Cataloguing in Publication Data is available.

Library of Congress Catalog Card Number: 2006003878
ISBN: 1-59158-358-6

First published in 2006

Libraries Unlimited/Teacher Ideas Press, 88 Post Road West, Westport, CT 06881
A Member of the Greenwood Publishing Group, Inc.
www.lu.com

Printed in the United States of America

The paper used in this book complies with the
Permanent Paper Standard issued by the National
Information Standards Organization (Z39.48–1984).

10 9 8 7 6 5 4 3 2 1

To my first chess teacher—Dr. Loren Schmidt,
Heritage University;

and

To my chess in education mentor—Dr. Tim Redman,
the University of Texas at Dallas

CONTENTS

Foreword *by Dr. John D. McNeil*   ix

♟ Chapter 1 Curriculum Orientations and
                 Organizing Elements   1
Introduction   1
Four Curriculum Orientations   4
Organizing Elements   6

♟ Chapter 2 Flow   7
Characteristics of the Flow Experience   7
Activities That Lead to Flow   9
Young People and Flow   10

♟ Chapter 3 Competition   13
General Principles   13
Recommendations   16
Who Plays Chess?   20
Pairings   26

♟ **Chapter 4** Sacrifice   29
Moral Development   29
Chess in Literature   31
Reading List   37

♟ **Chapter 5** Problem Solving   41
Content or General Heuristics?   41
Teacher Directed or Constructivist?   43

♟ **Chapter 6** Multiple Intelligences (MI)   47
Expertise   47
Spatial Intelligence   49
Bodily Kinesthetic Intelligence   50

♟ **Chapter 7** Planning   53
The Self-Directed Curriculum   53
Chess as Lifelong Learning   56
Smothered Mate Chess Game   58

♟ **Chapter 8** Lesson Plans   61
Third-Grade Beginner Plans   61
Sample Plans for Other Grades   73

Appendix A   State Standards   85

Appendix B   Chess Worksheets with Answer Keys   95

Glossary   101

Resources and References   109

Index   119

FOREWORD

Children and Chess: A Guide for Educators is a groundbreaking resource guide for teachers by Dr. Alexey Root, a curriculum specialist, renowned chess expert, and as shown in this text, one who practices abundance teaching—sharing ideas for wide application and making them accessible to all.

There are many other books that may encourage teachers to exercise will and skill in curriculum making and there are scores of activity booklets but few that connect their featured activity to long-range goals and offer such rich illustrations and explanations for practices that enhance the cognitive and academic growth of children by engaging them in chess at their appropriate developmental level, motivating them, and absorbing them in concentration.

More than that, prospective readers of this guide need not think of themselves as either experienced curriculum designers or knowledgeable about chess. The clarity of the writing, the numerous examples of teacher planning (drawn from the author's own experiences and from teachers who are working in a variety of contexts) have made *Children and Chess* a self-teaching tool for teachers. Interwoven are interesting stories that embellish knowledge about the game and presentations of current research findings about the learning process that explain how and why chess is a good vehicle for stimulating and channeling the emotions toward intellectual development.

Teachers at different grade levels and workers with mixed after-school groups will appreciate the scaffolding of plans for beginners as well as plans for the more advanced. The text speaks to those who seek alternatives to scripted lessons and recitations and who are looking for opportunities for themselves and for their students to use their imaginations. Particularly noteworthy, however, is how Dr. Root confronts realities of the standards-based curriculum by showing how the joy and play in chess transfers to acquiring the privileged content of the standards. Indeed both teachers and students will welcome the placement of chess as a different kind of learning opportunity, making the classroom environment more enjoyable and rewarding.

About fifteen years ago, Dr. Root was a graduate student in my curriculum course, and even then she showed the ability to see more than meets the eye, knowing that Yesterday's games give Today's strengths for Tomorrow's possibilities. She has continued to combine her curriculum scholarship with a passion for chess enabling her to offer *Children and Chess*—a treasure for those interested in creating challenging activities for helping children learn new skills, focus on the task at hand, and anticipate the thinking of others.

Dr. John D. McNeil
Professor Emeritus
Graduate School of Education & Information Studies UCLA

Chapter 1

CURRICULUM ORIENTATIONS AND ORGANIZING ELEMENTS

Introduction

Children and Chess: A Guide for Educators instructs educators on the reasons and the methods for including chess in their classrooms. Chess has much to offer for students in grades 3–8. Chess enables experiences of deep concentration, sharpens competitive skills, activates **multiple intelligences**, and allows students to experience sacrifice, problem solving, and planning. Psychological, curricular, and chess terms in **boldface** are defined in the glossary. Such terms are in boldface the first time they are used, in regular typeface thereafter. In *Children and Chess*, teachers have access to detailed chess lesson plans. By studying the plans in advance of using them with students, teachers can learn enough chess to teach the game. Other resources for teachers—such as software and chess books—are listed in Resources and References. Also in the back of the book are two appendixes: Appendix A lists state standards, and Appendix B contains chess worksheets (with answer keys).

Teachers may be reluctant to include chess in their classrooms because of perceived constraints on their curriculum choices. Yearly rounds of state tests, mandated curriculum standards, and ideas from other teachers, parents, and administrators about content all influence teachers' decision making. Some of the lesson plans in this book reference the TEKS, Texas Essential Knowledge and Skills (http://www.tea.state.tx.us). The TEKS are representative of states' expectations for students. In Appendix A, the

TEKS cited in the text are compared to other states' standards. Including state standards in lesson plans alleviates some concerns regarding the relationship of chess to scholastic requirements.

There are additional justifications for classroom time on chess. Cognitive psychologist Adriaan D. de Groot stated that, although it is true that most high-level skills (in music, mathematics, and chess) consist of very specific repertoires, instructing children in the basics of chess may promote transferable outcomes. Through minimal chess instruction, all students gain the important idea of *thinking before taking action.* Also, chess serves as another area where problem-solving rules apply. What follows is a brief summary of de Groot's ideas for optimally presenting chess curricula:

- Chess instruction requires relatively little time and should be given in the higher grades of elementary school by the best available methods and teachers, with modest educational objectives in mind.
- Chess serves as another area where problem-solving rules apply. Through exposure to problem solving in more than one subject matter, general **heuristics** will be more likely to be learned by pupils.
- Unique learning effects of chess could be sought. Those effects might be in non-cognitive areas, and might be for some pupils rather than all.

Other arguments in favor of chess may include

1. There is great enthusiasm for chess among schoolchildren of many nations.
2. Chess is a cultural institution.
3. Chess has inspired literature, the study of cognitive processes, and the development of artificial intelligence models.
4. Chess helps us recognize and deal with differences among individuals, and with winning and losing.
5. Like physical education, chess is a training field, without the pressure to perform academically (de Groot, 1981).

You may teach chess more at the start of the year, to acquaint students with the rules. As the year progresses, a few of your students may gravitate to your chess sets and boards. Chess games may start because of student initiative rather than your direction. Alternatively, you may find ways to harness chess to your educational purposes throughout the school year. The lesson plans in this book show how chess can be used to enhance reading, math, and problem solving. As you read this book, learn chess, and see how chess affects your students, you may be inspired to write more lesson plans that include chess. Or you may decide to start an extracurricular chess club. This guide will help you with any additional steps you wish to take with chess.

The lesson plans in this book were written either by me or by my online students. From 2001 until 2006, I taught a UT TeleCampus (http://www.telecampus.utsystem.edu) course called Chess in the Classroom. Most of my students were prospective or practicing classroom teachers. During the 16 weeks spent in my online classroom, my students learned how the spatial, logical, and social nature of chess could be used in their curricula. The course occasionally enrolled **tournament** chess players, but the majority of my online students were chess novices.

My own life has included playing chess, teaching (both academic subjects and chess), and raising my two children. I've been a tournament chess player since I was 9 years old. My most notable chess accomplishment was winning the U.S. Women's championship in 1989, the same year I married **International Master** and scientist Doug Root. During the late 1980s, I was a full-time public high school teacher (social studies and English). In the 1990s, I was a substitute teacher for all grades, and a chess teacher (at recreation centers, schools, chess camps, and private lessons). Since 1999, I've been a senior lecturer at the University of Texas at Dallas (UTD). In addition to teaching my online chess course, I have taught UTD education classes, tutored prospective teachers for certification exams, recruited students for the top-ranked UTD Chess Program, and supervised student teachers. During the last seven years, I've been a volunteer chess teacher at my children's schools (Figure 1.1).

My UCLA graduate school professors, in particular John D. McNeil, influenced the reading I did to prepare my online course and this guide. McNeil's *Contemporary Curriculum in Thought and Action* led me to works by Mihaly Csikszentmihalyi (pronounced chick-SENT-me-high) and Howard Gardner. Thus, you will find references to **flow** (a Csikszentmihalyi concept) and to Gardner's multiple intelligences. And, from McNeil, I borrowed **organizing elements**: the themes, concepts, generalizations, skills, and philosophical values that ground curricula. Some examples of organizing elements in this book are competition and problem solving.

The emphasis in this guide is on integrating chess examples with **academic** and **humanistic** goals. Benjamin Franklin believed that chess strengthened Foresight, Circumspection, Caution, and Perseverance. In that philosophical tradition, I propose that Flow, Competition, Sacrifice, Problem Solving, Multiple Intelligences, and Planning can be enhanced through incorporating chess in the classroom. The first seven chapters of this book define these concepts as organizing elements and show how they (and chess) can be integral

Figure 1.1

Alexey Root teaching chess to third graders.
Photo by Sondra Wilkerson.

parts of your classroom. Chapter 8 features lesson plans that you can use with your students. The section titled Resources and References lists outside resources about chess, for you to enhance your own chess knowledge. Also listed in Resources and References are the references for this text. Completing the book are the glossary; Appendix A, which lists state reading and math standards that might be addressed through chess; and Appendix B, which contains chess worksheets (with answer keys).

In this chapter, McNeil's curriculum framework is discussed. Teachers are important curriculum makers. One example of the academic curriculum orientation is Gardner's theory of multiple intelligences. The relationship of humanistic curriculum goals to the game of chess is briefly considered. Flow is an example of a humanistic curriculum goal.

Four Curriculum Orientations

Creativity constitutes the art of teaching. As McNeil (2006) wrote, "The teacher is a crucial maker of curriculum policy. Even in such a seemingly clear-cut subject as elementary arithmetic, the teacher is not simply an implementer of policy. Teachers decide whether to spend time on drill or problem solving" (p. 227). With the freedom to select classroom activities comes the responsibility to plan thoughtfully. McNeil described four curriculum orientations: **social reconstructionist**, **systemic**, academic, and humanistic.

Social Reconstructionist

Social reconstructionist curriculum acts for change in schools and society. Teachers encourage students to recognize that curriculum content has political meaning and serves particular interest groups. Students also take action. At one public middle school, the Los Angeles Leadership Academy, "Students hone their learning skills and academic knowledge by actively engaging in social protests aimed at securing better working conditions for marginalized peoples" (McNeil, 2006, p. 26).

Social adaptationist curriculum prepares students for current problems, for example AIDS prevention curriculum and anti-drug programs. Unlike social reconstruction, social adaptation does not develop critical consciousness in students. McNeil (2006, p. 34) wrote, "The approach of social adaptationists is to give students information and prescriptions for dealing with situations as defined rather than to seek a fundamental change in the basic structure of the society underlying the problems."

Systemic

Systemic curriculum "task-analyzes" objectives so that each step toward mastery is reinforced. Mastery learning is one systemic curriculum. "Instructional objectives, arranged in an assumed hierarchy of tasks, are the

Figure 1.2
Practicing chess.

keystone of the system, and lesson materials are built around that arrangement. The objectives are the intended outcomes of instruction" (McNeil, 2006, p. 50).

Academic

In this guide, academic and humanistic curricula are developed. Within the academic orientation, the "forms of knowledge" approach is taken. Philip H. Phenix, Paul Hirst, and Howard Gardner have separately proposed that each academic **domain** has its own "concepts, rules, and criteria for claims to truth" (McNeil, 2006, p. 64). Students should "acquire both substantive knowledge that has significance for them and knowledge of the general principles and ways of thinking that are the inherent features of the forms by which knowledge is gained" (McNeil, 2006, p. 64). Gardner (1999) favored exploring a small number of topics in depth, to increase understanding of concepts. Gardner's multiple intelligences (MI) theory respects the division of academia into different domains. Students may master a domain in about a decade, over thousands of hours of practice (Gardner, 1999, p. 119). Figure 1.2 shows a girl memorizing a chess **opening**.

MI theory states that students can use the eight different intelligences to become expert in the domains. Spatial intelligence activities, such as chess, may help students advance in reading and mathematics. MI theory provides a framework for chess to be a part of how students achieve academic goals.

Humanistic

Humanistic goals will also be featured in this guide. "Humanists believe that the function of the curriculum is to provide each learner with intrinsically rewarding experiences that contribute to personal liberation and development" (McNeil, 2006, p. 5). For humanists, the process is more important than the product. Especially valued are peak experiences, which (as in Figure 1.3) "give rise to love, hate, anxiety, depression, and joy. For [humanistic psychologist Abraham] Maslow, the peak experiences of awe, mystery, and wonder are both the end and the beginning of learning" (McNeil, 2006, p. 14).

Chess may lead to peak experiences. Chess often engages students' emotions. Within a single game,

Figure 1.3
Mountain climbing: A peak experience.

students may anticipate the joy of winning or the despair of losing. Emotion energizes intellect as students struggle to solve each chess position.

Organizing Elements

Definition

Academic and humanistic curriculum goals may be met through chess. Goals can be broken down into organizing elements. Organizing elements can be themes, concepts, generalizations, skills, or philosophical values (Figure 1.4).

McNeil (2006, p. 148) wrote,

Understanding organizing elements is a distinguishing attribute of the curriculum expert. A child may be immediately aware of learning activities or centers only in their concrete form, but the insightful teacher or curriculum writer is always conscious of their deeper significance. When one asks children what they are learning, they are likely to respond, "We're learning about Indians" or "We're learning to speak a foreign language." The curriculum person, however, sees, in addition to such direct study, the powerful abstractions to which the activity points. The activity dealing with Indians may be pointing toward a generalization about basic needs that all people have always had. Learning to speak a foreign language may be most important for what it illuminates about the student's own language, language in general, language acquisition, and even some more fundamental elements such as communication among people.

Examples

In this guide, six organizing elements are considered: flow (Chapter 2), competition (Chapter 3), sacrifice (Chapter 4), problem solving (Chapter 5), multiple intelligences (Chapter 6), and planning (Chapter 7). For organizing elements in lesson plans, see Chapter 8. Specific objectives from TEKS (http://www.tea.state.tx.us) are used as examples of scholastic content throughout the text. In Appendix A, other states' standards are listed for comparison. Humanistic aspects of chess are illustrated by anecdotes and references to psychology in the chapters on flow, competition, sacrifice, and planning. Chess in the academic curriculum is discussed in the chapters on problem solving and multiple intelligences.

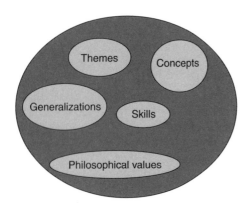

Figure 1.4
Organizing elements.

Chapter 2

FLOW

Humanistic psychologists Rollo May, Abraham Maslow, and Mihaly Csikszentmihalyi define what makes life enjoyable. Chess is a flow activity that develops habits of mind necessary for growth. Entropy, disorder, and chaos can be avoided by a mind trained in a symbolic language such as that of chess. Implications for all ages, but especially the young, are discussed.

Characteristics of the Flow Experience

Runner's High

The silence at scholastic chess tournaments fascinates observers. Rows of children quietly contemplate the **pieces** and **pawns** in front of them. These moments of complete absorption are very unlike the stereotypical frenetic image of children. Consider this chess tournament report from the *Lincoln Journal-Star* (Beutler, 1995, p. 20):

> If you could hear them think, the room would explode with sound. Instead, a quiet prevails, punctuated by the click of time **clock**s and the occasional declaration of "**check**" as players **move** to trap their opponents. This is the stuff of serious play. And fun. [boldface added; see glossary for terms' definitions]

Figure 2.1

Aha!

Sitting still, chess players nonetheless experience a "runner's high." Measurements taken of chess players show similar changes to those of athletes, artists, and ordinary people experiencing "moments of intensive encounter." Those changes include "quickened heart beat; higher blood pressure; increased intensity and constriction of vision" (May, 1975, p. 44; see also Kriz, Vokal, & Krizova [1990], which compares heart rates of hockey players and chess players).

Self Actualization

Changes in physiological measurements, such as those experienced by chess players during games, may be felt as joy. May (1975, p. 45) defined joy as the feeling that comes with actualizing one's potentialities. In an interview, chess **master** Bruce Pandolfini said, "When you're looking at a position and thinking for a long time, and don't have the answer but you don't give up, you stay with it and stay with it, then when it hits you, that you're about to get it, it's so invigorating, it raises you to another level. . . . That is the most exciting moment" (Killigrew, 2000b, p. 39). (See Figure 2.1.) Similarly, Maslow (1968, pp. 106–107) described persons during peak experiences as feeling like the creators of their own destinies, with more control than at other life moments.

Satisfaction

McNeil (2006, p. 14) wrote,

Believing in the need to discover one's potentials and limitations through intense activity, Mihaly Csikszentmihalyi . . . began his studies of optimal and enjoyable experiences in which there is a deep concentration on the activity at hand—the person forgetting his or her problems and temporarily losing the awareness of self. Such experiences are termed "flow."

According to Csikszentmihalyi (1990), flow is what enables people to be satisfied with, and have a sense of exercising control in, their lives. How we internally order the chaos of life, our subjective experience, "is life itself" (Csikszentmihalyi, 1990, pp. 192–193).

Activities That Lead to Flow

Chess is one of Csikszentmihalyi's exemplars of an activity designed for flow: "The way a long-distance swimmer felt when crossing the English Channel was almost identical to the way a chess player felt during a tournament or a climber progressing up a difficult rock face" (Csikszentmihalyi, 1990, p. 48); "games, sports, and artistic and literary forms were developed over the centuries for the express purpose of enriching life with enjoyable experiences" (Csikszentmihalyi, 1990, p. 51; see also p. 72). Flow experiences are most similar to the feeling of "designing or discovering something new" (Csikszentmihalyi, 1990, p. 256).

Eight Components of Flow Activities

According to Csikszentmihalyi (1990, p. 49), flow activities (a) give the chance of completion, (b) require concentration, (c) have clear goals, (d) provide immediate feedback, (e) remove the participant from the worries of everyday life, (f) require participants to exercise control, (g) strengthen the sense of self, and (h) alter the sense of the duration of time.

■ *Chess as a flow exemplar*

Csikszentmihalyi uses chess to illustrate the eight major components of flow. Regarding letters (c) and (d), "the chess player's goals are equally obvious: to **mate** the opponent's **king** before his own is mated. With each move, he can calculate whether he has come closer to this objective" (Csikszentmihalyi, 1990, p. 54; bold added to indicate glossary listings). Regarding letter (e), "if a person loses a chess game . . . he need not worry. . . . Thus the flow experience is typically described as involving a sense of control—or, more precisely, as lacking the sense of worry about losing control that is typical in many situations of normal life" (p. 59). And regarding letter (g),

> In a chess tournament, players whose attention has been riveted, for hours, to the logical battle on the board claim that they feel as if they have been merged into a powerful "field of force" clashing with other forces in some nonmaterial dimension of existence. (pp. 64–65)

Life as a Game

Life is more enjoyable if subjectively structured like a game. Humanistic psychologists such as Erik Erikson, Abraham Maslow, and Lawrence Kohlberg define stages or steps in human development (McNeil, 2006, pp. 160–161; Csikszentmihalyi, 1990, pp. 221–223, 278). "From this point of view, individual life appears to consist of a series of different 'games,' with different goals and challenges, that change with time as a person matures" (Csikszentmihalyi, 1990, p. 223). Specific fields within life can also be per-

ceived as games. For example, a physicist described the development of quantum physics as "a game, a very interesting game one could play" (Csikszentmihalyi, 1990, p. 135). Also, "the more a job inherently resembles a game—with variety, appropriate and flexible challenges, clear goals, and immediate feedback—the more enjoyable it will be regardless of the worker's level of development" (Csikszentmihalyi, 1990, p. 152).

Figure 2.2

Young people playing a chess tournament.

Young People and Flow

Mastering a harmonious system of symbols (like art, music, physics, or chess) is one path to flow. Mastery buffers the young child or early teen against the angst of a "pimple erupting on the chin, or a friend ignoring him at school" (Csikszentmihalyi, 1990, p. 202). By knowing how to internally order life's chaos, a skill that can be learned though chess, a young person can cope with external disappointments. (See Figure 2.2.)

Avoiding Chaos

Chess helps one avoid the normal condition of entropy—of having one's attention being attracted to what is problematic at the moment (Csikszentmihalyi, 1990, p. 119). "Games fill out the interludes of the cultural script. They enhance action and concentration during 'free time,' when cultural instructions offer little guidance, and a person's attention threatens to wander into the uncharted realms of chaos" (Csikszentmihalyi, 1990, p. 81).

Humorist Art Buchwald (1993, p. 111) wrote about learning chess at the Hebrew Orphan Asylum summer camp, commenting that the game helped him through many tough times, including a stint with the Marines. Buchwald said that playing chess when stationed in the Pacific helped pass the time, especially during slow periods.

Escaping Loneliness

Watching TV, taking drugs, or engaging in criminal mischief to escape one's loneliness and disappointments is easier than mastering a symbolic system such as chess (Csikszentmihalyi, 1990, pp. 30, 69, 169, 170). Csikszentmihalyi recognizes this problem, and suggests a solution:

> Many children never reach the point of recognizing the possibilities of the activity into which they are forced, and end up disliking it forever. How many children have come to hate classical music because their parents forced them to practice an instrument? Often children—and adults—need external incentives to take the first steps in an activity that requires a difficult restructuring of attention. Most enjoyable activities are not natural; they demand an effort that initially one is reluctant to make. But once the interaction starts to provide feedback to the person's skills, it usually begins to be intrinsically rewarding. (p. 68)

Controlling Consciousness

For the young, chess is an early lesson in how to control consciousness. Adolescents who fail to learn such habits of mind grow up to become undisciplined adults. Adults, too, need a hobby like chess to "control attention in solitude" and turn away from "whatever dulls or distracts the mind." In old age, when "physical vigor fails," one will be ready to "read Proust, take up chess, grow orchids, help one's neighbors, and think about God—if these are the things one has decided are worth pursuing" (Csikszentmihalyi, 1990, p. 172). Though it's best to acquire habits such as chess early, acquisition at any age means that favorable external conditions are not necessary to enjoy life:

> It does not matter where one starts—whether one chooses goals first, develops skills, cultivates the ability to concentrate, or gets rid of self-consciousness. One can start anywhere, because once the flow experience is in motion the other elements will be much easier to attain. (Csikszentmihalyi, 1990, p. 212)

Chapter 3

COMPETITION

Based on your learners or on school policy, competitive chess games among children may be inappropriate during classes. Chess competition entails all games where results are tallied. Losers sometimes cry, and reasons for their tears are discussed. In this chapter, I offer two activities (reviewing competition games and physical conditioning) and three reasons (achieving one's best, creativity, and art) why chess competition is beneficial. Gifted and special needs, female and male, high- and low-rated, and computer chess players are discussed. The many categories of players allows for a variety of **pairing** (who plays against whom) arrangements.

General Principles

Competitive situations exist in school and in youth sports. According to research, school tests and P.E. interclass volleyball games cause as much stress as extracurricular team sports (Martens, 1982, p. 205).

Individual Events

Individual events (such as gymnastics, band solo performance, and wrestling) are more stressful for children than team sports. That is, before the competitive event, the participants in individual events reported more nervousness and jittery feelings than those about to play a team competition (Passer, 1982, pp. 158–165).

Figure 3.1

Team tournament.

■ *Chess as an exemplar of an individual event*

Chess is most often an individual event. One child plays against another, and the ultimate winner of the tournament is the child who racks up the most **points**. A child may score a **win**, a **loss**, or a **draw** (tie) in any particular game. A win is worth one point, a draw is worth 1/2 point, and a loss is worth 0 points.

In nontournament situations, a pair or threesome of children might play another pair or threesome of children. Each group privately consults and then makes an agreed-upon move against the other group. In this way, as the game is going on, verbal interactions and explanations within each pair or threesome enhance learning. In contrast, consulting books, computers, or friends is forbidden during tournament rounds. Analogies for the difference between consultation chess play compared to tournament games include study groups vs. individual tests and theater rehearsal (on book) vs. performance (off book).

In tournament play, even when teams of children play matches against other teams, the games are one-on-one (Figure 3.1). That is, one team's top-ranked player plays the top player on the other team, the second best plays the second best, and so on.

Chess and Crying

At the SuperNationalsII 2001, the largest (4,400 schoolchildren) K–12 chess tournament held up to that date in the United States, I asked parents and coaches whether their chess participants had cried or become very upset. Twenty-one respondents indicated that crying or severe upset had occurred among their young charges at the present or at the immediately preceding tournament; 39 respondents said that such incidents had not happened in the current or immediately preceding tournament. Two categories emerged as reasons for crying: children's preparation and the structure of chess tournaments (Root, December 2001).

■ *Children's preparation*

With regard to preparation, the adult respondents mentioned the following about different crying children: "[he] didn't recognize the [chess] opening and wasn't sure how to respond"; "the chess board not being set up properly and noticing too late to do anything about it"; "my six-year-old son was not upset that he lost but that he made a mistake and got distracted in his **notation**." At SuperNationalsII and other rated scholastic chess competitions, noticing illegal starting positions or moves is the responsibility of the chess competitors. With the exception of games played with less than 29 minutes per side, participants in scholastic chess tournaments must take notation (Barber, 2003, p. 27). Thus, in these cases of crying, it seemed that the individual child's abilities did not match the requirements of competitive scholastic chess games.

In other words, these chess children cried because they weren't prepared. Engh (1999, p. 149) cited the National Youth Sports Coaches' survey regarding the preparation deficit among youth sports competitors: 49% of 1,100 children in the age range of 5 to 8 lacked the minimal skill level to be successful in their sport.

■ *Tournament structure*

Scholastic chess tournament structure contributed to other cases of crying or severe upset. The actions of **tournament directors (TDs)** and rewards for chess are mentioned in these respondents' remarks: One woman noted that "my son was told to wait in one area for the start of a tournament. I noticed other children were starting to play, and sent him over there. The TD told my son he wasn't seated in time, and would be forfeited. My son cried." A 12-year-old boy, as quoted by his parent, said, "There goes my chance for a scholarship."

■ *Tournament directors*

TD behavior is problematic in scholastic chess. As recently as 1998 in Texas, many scholastic TDs wore no identifying badges, hats, or uniforms. Furthermore, some scholastic events had multiple unmonitored entrances and exits. As a concerned parent, I noted that my then 5-year-old could have wandered off into the second floor of a downtown Dallas hotel during the 1998 Pan-American Scholastic chess tournament (Root, March/April, 1999).

Awareness of security issues has improved since then, but other concerns remain. Kiewra & Igo (2001) noted that little attention is paid to the noise level in scholastic chess. At national championship scholastic events, "Spectators routinely milled around the playing area and socialized. Scores of spectators channeled past some players every minute—so close they brushed or bumped them" (Kiewra & Igo, p. 1). TDs failed to control the noise, and sometimes even talked loudly themselves within earshot of ongoing games. Kiewra points out the problem with such distractions: "No matter how hard players try to concentrate and calculate, attention is involuntarily diverted to other attention demanding stimuli such as movement, loud noises, and even whispers" (p. 4). Referring to the same SuperNationalsII at which my crying research was conducted, Kiewra noted that the players all competed in one large room, and spectators roller-skated and played hacky sack within feet of competitive scholastic chess games. Comparing chess games to tests taken at school, Kiewra concluded, "Educational psychologists know that preparation alone casts a dim light. Students and chess players must fully concentrate when tested in the classroom or at the chess board. Teachers and tournament officials must help by taking steps to minimize distractions. Only then, can students and chess players think and calculate to their full potentials" (p. 9).

■ *Rewards*

There is lively debate in chess and in sports about the efficacy of trophies. Robert Musicant said that many children play chess just to get a trophy. He argued that this love of trophies meant that children avoid informal games, which don't have trophy rewards. And, without frequent informal practice, Musicant believed that the children had little hope of improving their chess abilities. Since trophies as awards are rare in open (as opposed to scholastic) tournaments, such children left competitive chess once they became too old for scholastic chess (Musicant, 2001, p. 54). Keith Storey responded that increasing trophy reinforcement is important until students reach a level of competence that is satisfying in itself (Storey, 2001, p. 52).

Youth sports have no definitive answers regarding the effects of awards for winners. "All Star" games are disappearing in some youth sports. Some leagues keep score on the sidelines, rather than the scoreboard. Instead of awarding trophies to the top teams or scorers, sportsmanship and participation medals are distributed to all competitors.

Recommendations

Paying attention to children's chess preparation and improving conditions at chess tournaments are both actions that are worth pursuing. "The manner in which coaches structure the athletic situation, the goal priorities they establish explicitly and implicitly, and the ways in which they relate to their players can markedly influence how children appraise the situation and the amount of stress they experience" (Smith & Smoll, 1982, p. 183). Books on how to improve children's chess preparation are available from the online catalog of the **United States Chess Federation (USCF)** (http://www.uscfsales.com/). Helpful for understanding the structure of scholastic chess tournaments is Dewain Barber's (2003) free pamphlet *A Guide to Scholastic Chess*. For ideas about enhancing child development through competition, a coaching book such as *Children in Sport* by Magill, Ash, & Smoll (1982) would be appropriate. Volunteering to help at chess tournaments, or becoming a TD oneself, are viable options for the concerned teacher or parent.

Even with excellent preparation and good tournament conditions, children may cry after losing chess games. Crying may be an expression of a competitive desire to excel. Robert McKenzie, math specialist at Castle Hill Elementary, wrote about crying on the discussion board for my online chess course:

If I have a student who still cries after a loss [even after I prepared him chess content-wise and told him that losing some games is inevitable], I would console him and tell him it is OK and offer to review his game if needed. Or, if he didn't write the game out, I would go over some more ideas with him. I would tell him that he should not worry because there will plenty of games in the future to play. In addition, sometimes I share my personal stories of losing and overcoming; this sometimes lets them know that there is hope for them to improve and win later on in the future. Personally I don't think crying is always a bad thing; sometimes crying shows me that a student is very serious about wanting to be good and I think crying is just an expression of that. To just say to a child that "hey it's OK to lose and that just playing the game is all that is important" is a little misleading. In life people get fired for repeatedly losing. Even in teaching, if your children don't pass the test it does not matter that you taught your best, you will still be fired. Coaching is the same way; it depends on your goals. The other day I saw this 7-foot basketball player crying on TV because his team was losing. I think his coach appreciates that emotion and knows that his player wants to win. I know with me flow is achieved much quicker for me when I win at chess. When I lose I still get mad. This losing pushes me to get better.

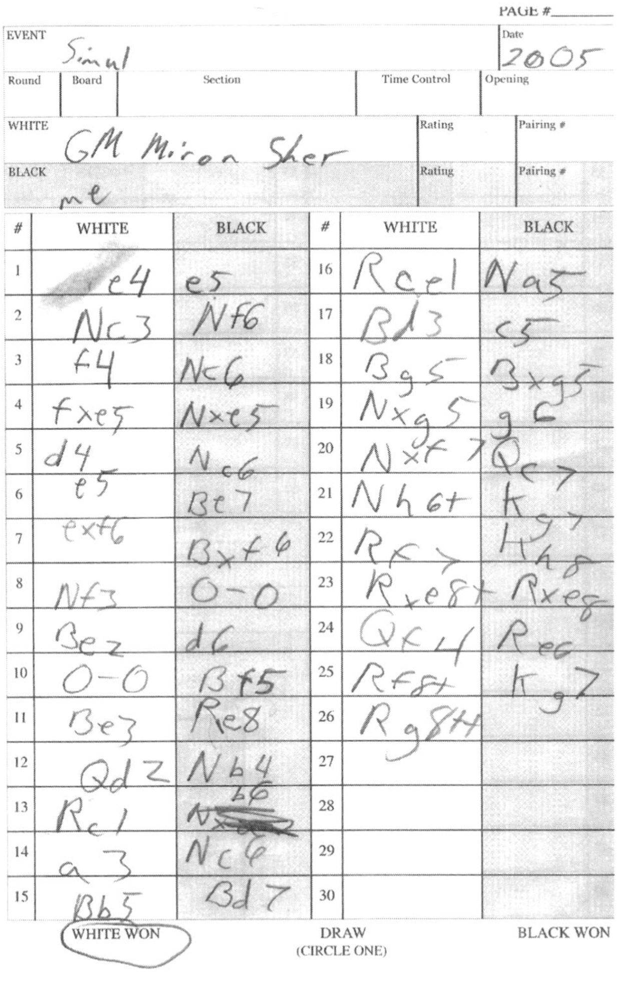
PAGE #

EVENT Simul | Date 2005

Round | Board | Section | Time Control | Opening

WHITE GM Miron Sher | Rating | Pairing #

BLACK me | Rating | Pairing #

#	WHITE	BLACK	#	WHITE	BLACK
1	e4	e5	16	Re1	Na5
2	Nc3	Nf6	17	Bd3	c5
3	f4	Nc6	18	Bg5	Bxg5
4	fxe5	Nxe5	19	Nxg5	g6
5	d4	Nc6	20	Nxf7	Qe7
6	e5	Be7	21	Nh6+	Kg7
7	exf6	Bxf6	22	Rf7	Kh8
8	Nf3	O-O	23	Rxe8+	Rxe8
9	Be2	d6	24	Qf4	Re6
10	O-O	Bf5	25	Rf8+	Kg7
11	Be3	Re8	26	Rg8+	
12	Qd2	Nb4	27		
13	Re1	b6	28		
14	a3	Nc6	29		
15	Bb5	Bd7	30		

WHITE WON DRAW (CIRCLE ONE) BLACK WON

Figure 3.2

Chess notation score sheet.

Reviewing Competition Games

In the previous paragraph, McKenzie refers to reviewing competition games with students. Perhaps the most important strategy for both improving my **chess rating** and continuing my affection for chess and chess players has been analyzing my tournament games with my opponents. In chess competitions and exhibitions, the review process is facilitated by a game **score sheet** (Figure 3.2). The notation written on a score sheet is a record of the game's moves. The pictured score sheet is from a **simultaneous** game played in 2005 by **Grandmaster** Miron Sher versus my daughter Clarissa. Sher played about 35 youngsters during that 2-hour exhibition, losing just one of his simultaneous games.

Playing over your notated game with your opponent allows the two of you to recollect and to share your thoughts about the completed game. If there are notation errors on the score sheet, you can help each other reconstruct what moves were actually played. This review session is called a **postmortem**. Postmortems can establish a learning and social context. You and your opponent confer: "This is our game that we created together. What can we learn from it?" During postmortems you socialize with your opponent, and this social context is pleasurable. "All the studies . . . confirm the fact that simply being with other people generally improves a person's mood significantly, regardless of what else is happening" (Csikszentmihalyi, 1990, p. 251).

A practical coach reviews each player's games with that player, perhaps during a coaching session after the particular tournament concludes (Figure 3.3). Other effective techniques include teaching principles of chess and giving specific chess drills—such as **chess problems, speed chess,** and **blindfold chess** (Horgan & Morgan, 1990, pp. 125–126).

Keeping notation, reviewing games, and other chess drills may improve success in school. Winner (1996, p. 307) noted that musical children may do well in school because they learn music notation. She felt that this musical skill generalized to academic requirements and that the daily practice required by music imparts discipline. Similarly, one could argue that chess competitors' routines of notating games and chess drills are compatible with school demands.

Physical Conditioning

Physical fitness is important for chess success. Csikszentmihalyi (1990) wrote,

Figure 3.3

Alexey Root reviews a game with high school chess players. Copyright 2005 Bob Lindholm.

Most mental activities also rely on the physical dimension. Chess, for instance, is one of the most cerebral games there is; yet advanced chess players train by running and swimming because they are aware that if they are physically unfit they will not be able to sustain the long periods of mental concentration that chess tournaments require. (p. 118)

I have been a competitive swimmer, off and on, since I was 8 years old. Swimming is helpful for my chess game, and satisfying in its own right. At tournaments in the year 2000, I swam alongside Grandmaster Arthur Bisguier, age 70+, and the 2000 National Elementary Champion (later the 2005 U.S. Chess Champion), Hikaru Nakamura.

FIDE World Champion Viswanathan Anand said,

Physical preparation is really important in order to reach my level now. I have paid more attention to this aspect in the last two years, and now I feel able to play for a whole month or two without collapsing or blundering due to lack of concentration. I keep the same level without much effort and my play has stability. I used to take long walks or do some swimming, but that was it. Now I spend two hours in the morning at the gym. (Llada, 2001)

Achieving One's Best

Csikszentmihalyi (1990) wrote the following about competition:

One simple way to find challenges is to enter a competitive situation. Hence the great appeal of all games and sports that pit a person or team against another. In many ways, competition is a quick way of developing complexity: "He who wrestles with us," wrote Edmund Burke, "strengthens our nerves, and sharpens our skill. Our antagonist is our helper." The challenges of competition can be stimulating and enjoyable. But when beating the opponent takes precedence in the mind over performing as well as possible, enjoyment tends to disappear. Competition is enjoyable only when it is a means to perfect one's skills; when it becomes an end in itself, it ceases to be fun. (p. 50)

Similarly, Pandolfini said,

Chess is competition. And there are good things about competition. Competition is only bad when you demean the other individual because of it. But there's nothing wrong with trying to win and excel, I have no problem with that. Where would civilization be if every individual didn't try to do his or her best? We'd be nowhere. (Killigrew, 2000a, p. 33)

Creativity

Besides sharpening students' skills through competition, chess games give students a chance to be creative. For higher-level chess players, recognized innovations are possible. "Chess is a very logical domain, and if anyone were to discover a new opening combination or effective **endgame**, the discovery would be instantly adopted by players all around the globe. . . . [Therefore] it is potentially easier to be creative in" chess than in other domains (Csikszentmihalyi, 1996, p. 339; bold added to indicate glossary reference).

The sheer number of moves also means that schoolchildren's games are unique (McCafferty, 1999). So, even though a schoolchild's "new" opening might not be favorably reviewed by grandmasters, it is a creative act for that child (Krogius & Gershunski, 1987).

Art

Competition in chess strips away our preconceived notions. Competitors do not memorize a game and play it out on the board. Each move causes players to reevaluate their plans, and (at some point in the game) to veer away from home-prepared lines. The resulting game is likely more original than what either player could have created alone. The competitive chess player is an original artist:

> Whereas a conventional artist starts painting a canvas knowing what she wants to paint, and holds to her original intention until the work is finished, an original artist with equal technical training . . . keeps modifying the picture in response to the unexpected colors and shapes emerging on the canvas, and ends up with a finished work that probably will not resemble anything she started out with. If the artist is responsive to her inner feelings, knows what she likes and does not like, and pays attention to what is happening on the canvas, a good painting is bound to emerge. (Csikszentmihalyi, 1990, p. 208)

Visual artist Marcel Duchamp once said, "All chess players are artists" (Humble, 1998, p. 43). P. N. Humble explained the appeal of chess to Duchamp as a forum for creating beautiful games. Recording wins was definitely secondary to chess artistry (p. 48).

Who Plays Chess?

Gifted

According to the research of Ellen Winner and others, global giftedness is rare (Winner, 1996, p. 307). It may be more common to be unequally gifted in math and verbal abilities than to be balanced between those two areas (Winner, 1996, p. 35). As discussed in Chapter 6, children may be gifted in one or more of the eight intelligences listed by Gardner. For example, mathematical prodigies fall into three categories: "those who use visual-spatial reasoning to solve math problems, those who use verbal strategies, and those who use both" (Winner, 1996, p. 48).

My own academic giftedness had notable imbalances. Just before my 14th birthday, I took the Washington Pre-College Test, a multiple-choice test similar to the SAT1. Compared to all high school students who took the test, I scored in the 98th percentile on both the verbal and quantitative composites. Yet I scored in the bottom 10th percentile in spatial ability and the bottom 20th percentile in mechanical reasoning.

All the tests were paper-and-pencil (two-dimensional). The spatial ability test baffled me: I could not imagine how to rotate shapes to match the prompt. For the mechanical reasoning test, I guessed at how moving one gear would affect an adjacent one.

More interesting than my test results is why I took those tests in 1979. I had competed in the U.S. Junior Open chess tournament, held at the University of Washington from July 31 to August 4, 1978. The only other girl in the tournament, Sharon Monohon, was housed on the same dorm floor as I. I had just turned 13, and she was a year or two older. Sharon told me that she was going to university next year, because of her advanced math ability. I could defeat her at chess, so I thought to myself, "I should get to go to university too!" When I came home from the Junior Open, I told my parents that I wanted to skip high school. My parents arranged for the appropriate tests, and by the next summer, I was set to matriculate in the fall of 1979. I ran into Sharon again, at another chess tournament. I asked her how college had gone for her in 1978–79. She replied, "Oh, I meant I was going next calendar year, not next school year." It turned out that she, too, was matriculating in the fall of 1979. Chess tournaments give a child intellectually motivated peers, who then inspire one another to early or advanced achievements.

Competing successfully against adults also encourages children intellectually. When I was 13, I was interviewed about my chess accomplishments by a local newspaper. Having competed successfully in both junior and adult chess tournaments, I told the reporter, "You come to realize that you can deal with adults on the same level" (Tucker, 1978).

Giftedness at chess does not mean uniform intellectual interests outside of chess. Some of the world champions, notably Philidor, Euwe, and Botvinnik, were widely respected in their other, non–chess-playing professions. Prior to the reign of Bobby Fischer (1972–1975), whose influence raised prize funds for the world championship, many chess champions had careers aside from chess. The chart in Figure 3.4 was adapted from Web site information written by Larry Parr (2005) and personal communication with International Master and *Los Angeles Times* chess columnist Jack Peters (2005). Champions listed as "chess professionals" made their living from chess: tournaments, matches, simultaneous exhibitions, coffeehouse wagers, writing (chess books and chess magazines), and chess tutoring. The term "world chess champion" didn't come into widespread use until Steinitz.

Because I reached an **expert** chess rating at the age of 15, I was considered gifted by the American Chess Foundation (now Chess-in-the-Schools, http://www.chessintheschools.org). My accomplishment was not unusual. Young teenagers become chess masters, and even children as young as 6 and 7 can compete with adults (Horgan, 1992, p. 44). Indeed, the chess prodigy often makes his mark before age 10. "Only in chess, music, and mathematics have profound, original insights been contributed by preadolescents. Reshevsky and Capablanca were executing highly original combinations before their ninth birthdays" (Cranberg & Albert, 1988, p. 167). Knowledge of the world isn't a prerequisite for success in chess, music, or mathematics. In contrast, to write a great novel one must be thoroughly acquainted with society.

Figure 3.4

World chess champions and their professions.

Champion	Lifespan	Title Years	Profession(s)
Philidor	1726–1795	1747–1795	Music composer and musician, in the employ of the King of France
Deschapelles	1780–1847	1800–1821	Whist (and other games) player
La Bourdonnais	1795–1840	1821–1840	Chess professional
Saint-Amant	1800–1872	1840–1843	Wine merchant, clerk, actor, explorer
Staunton	1810–1874	1843–1851	Shakespeare scholar, writer
Anderssen	1818–1879	1851–1858; 1862–1866	Mathematics and German language professor
Morphy	1837–1884	1858–1862	Lawyer
Steinitz	1836–1900	1886–1894	Chess professional
Lasker	1868–1941	1894–1921	Mathematics, philosophy, bridge
Capablanca	1888–1942	1921–1927	Diplomat/goodwill ambassador (Cuba); actor (*Chess Fever* film)
Alekhine	1892–1946	1927–1935; 1937–1946	Magistrate (some legal training), chess professional
Euwe	1901–1981	1935–1937	Doctorate in mathematics, World Chess Federation president
Botvinnik	1911–1995	1948–1957; 1958–1960; 1961–1963	Electrical engineer, computer programmer; established chess school
Smyslov	1921–	1957–1958	Opera singer
Tal	1936–1992	1960–1961	Chess professional
Petrosian	1929–1984	1963–1969	Chess professional
Spassky	1937–	1969–1972	Chess professional

Females and Males

At the high end of mathematical talent, Winner stated that there are differences between males and females in spatial ability (1996, p. 53). *The Wall Street Journal* reported that, in the United States in 2004, more than twice as many boys as girls scored higher than 700 on the math SAT—9.3% of boys versus 4.4% of girls (Whalen & Begley, 2005). Yet in England, the *Journal* article noted, the gender gap in math achievement is closing because of changes in the mathematics curriculum: eliminating gender stereotypes in textbooks; emphasizing analysis over timed, competitive problem solving; having students write down (instead of call out) answers; less lecturing and more visual and hands-on materials; and experimenting with single-sex math classrooms.

In an unpublished study of non-masters by D. Lane, there was no correlation between chess rating and performance on a spatial visualization task (Cranberg & Albert, 1988, p. 161). At least for non-masters, then, differences among females and males in chess potential may not be detectable by non-chess, visuospatial measures.

A counterview is proposed by Frydman and Lynn. Their hypothesis is that differences in spatial ability (as measured by a nonchess test) explain the small numbers of top female players. They tested 33 tournament-level Belgian chess players, aged 8 to 13. All scored above average (IQ 121; 100 is average) on the French Wechsler Intelligence Scale for Children. They scored particularly well (IQ 129) on the performance tasks, which included assembling puzzles and building block designs. Frydman and Lynn (1992) speculated that strong visuospatial skills are necessary for becoming a chess grandmaster. Thus, according the Frydman and Lynn (p. 235), male predominance in chess may be partially explained by gender differences in visuospatial abilities. Frydman and Lynn did not separate out the IQ results of the four chess-playing girls in their study.

The small number of female chess players, coupled with few research studies, makes drawing conclusions about chess and gender difficult. Few girls continue competing at chess as adults, thus diminishing greatly the pool of potential female masters and grandmasters. According to 1993 USCF statistics, less than 1% (.0085 = 612 women) of USCF's members over 21 were women (Lawrence, 1993). Wilgoren (2005) updated: "Of the U.S. Chess Federation's 82,500 members, 8.5 percent are female; among the adults, it is 2.3 percent." In the case of these latter statistics, "adult" may refer to over 18 rather than over 21. Gardner (1999) posits at least 10 years to master a domain. Aside from the World Champion title, being a grandmaster is the highest level of chess accomplishment. There are about 950 grandmasters, 11 of whom are female (Flora, 2005). Grandmaster results usually come after about 16 years (for those who learned chess rules at age 10 or under), and after about 12 years for those starting at age 12 or later (Krogius, 1976, p. 241). Most women play tournament chess for less than 10 years, and they are not keen chess participants. Charness and Gerchak (1996) found that "the difference in the number of keen participants in an activity can account for the difference in achievements" (p. 50). Based on their formula (which takes participation rates into account), the predicted gap between the top female and male is 172 rating points. On the FIDE (World Chess Federation) Web site (http://www.fide.com) in 2005, Judith Polgar (the top-rated female) was 76 rating points behind the top-rated male player.

One doctoral dissertation found that girls who start competitive chess at the same age as boys, and receive the same level of coaching, attain similar adult ratings. In a database of several hundred competitive chess players, the girls (on average) began competitive chess at age 14, whereas the boys (on average) began at age 9 (Gilbert, 1989).

Boys' greater interest in formal games may play a significant role in explaining their chess success. Differences have been found between boys and girls on the type of play preferred. In a study of fifth graders' recess, physical education, and after-school play, boys reported that 65% of their play activities were formal games. The girls played formal games 35% of the time. Moreover, girls who played boys' games may be called tomboys (Lever, 1976, p. 481).

To summarize the chess and gender studies, girls begin competitive chess later and play formal games less often than boys. There is a relatively small pool of female competitive chess players. These findings may explain most of the variance in chess achievement. Cranberg & Albert (1988, p. 159) thought that culture was at least as important as biology in explaining male ascendancy in chess.

Some, including me, have suggested that developing more female-only tournaments could provide social support for girls and women to stay in chess (Galitis, 2002). Historically, countries with separate women's events (such as Soviet Georgia) had greater female participation, and success, in chess than did the United States.

In the United States, gender-segregated events are rare. The U.S. Women's Championship was held as a women's-only invitational event from 1937 to 2001. It was sometimes held annually, though often just every second or third year. In 2002, the gender-segregated U.S. Women's Championship was abolished. Instead, the top women players in the country competed in a mixed (male and female) **Swiss system** 2002 U.S. Championship. The top female finisher in the 2002 U.S. Championship tournament was declared the U.S. Women's Chess Champion. Several regional women's championships have run annually for a few years and then disappeared. In 2004, Grandmaster Susan Polgar (oldest sister of Judith Polgar) established the Susan Polgar National Invitational for Girls (http://www.polgarchess.com). Its state qualifying system and culminating event at the U.S. Open are reigniting interest in single-sex events for girls. No equivalent event has been established for adult U.S. women.

Participation by rank-and-file female chess players in USCF events remains low. Because of the statistical underrepresentation of women in chess, *Chicago Tribune* columnist Eric Zorn (1997) suggested that having women's chess tournaments and champions was a good idea. He added that the occasional exceptions of women being top players showed that biology was not the inhibitor to chess achievement. Rather, he argued, women's underrepresentation was due to historically entrenched social factors and might best be addressed by affirmative action chess events and titles.

Differently Abled

■ *Deaf*

Being deaf is not considered a handicap in chess, and no special provisions are made for deaf tournament players. According to Jack Peters (personal communication, 2001), the result of the 1971 world championship qualifier in Seville, Spain, was affected by noise. When trailing by only a point (with 3 games left to play) in a best-of-10-games series, Robert Huebner resigned his Candidates match against Tigran Petrosian. Huebner complained that the noise from pedestrians overhead (the match was played in a basement just below street level) distracted him, and that the organizers did not do enough to improve the conditions. Petrosian didn't complain; he turned off his hearing aid.

■ *Blind*

Separate tournaments for the blind are

conducted with peg-in boards. White pieces have pointed tops, Black tops are rounded. A. F. Mackenzie, the most famous blind problemist, said in 1902: "I have lately come to think that problem composition is peculiarly a mental work, and that employment of board and men is in many ways a nuisance. . . . Certainly the three-movers I composed since losing my sight are infinitely superior, as a whole, to those composed before." (Evans, 2000, p. 13)

■ *Prodigies and savants*

Some evidence exists that neither high general **intelligence** nor high visual-spatial intelligence is necessary to play chess. Winner (1996. p. 33) cited a study of prodigies by David Feldman and Lynn Goldsmith. That study found prodigies performing at adult levels in chess and a few other domains, but acting as average children on tasks outside their areas of talent. Savants, who are individuals with low general intelligence performing at spectacular levels in formal domains, have been found in chess (Winner, 1996, p. 307).

Gardner considered Bobby Fischer, the World Chess Champion, as somewhat of a savant (Linton Productions, 1995). Cranberg & Albert (1988, p. 160) stated, "Bobby Fischer has been rumored to have an IQ in the 180s," but they also noted the need for "careful studies of the intelligence or nonchess intellectual capabilities of top-flight chess players." After reviewing the limited studies done on the intellectual capabilities of chess players, Cranberg & Albert concluded that "remarkable chess skill can exist in isolation, unaccompanied by other noteworthy intellectual abilities" (p. 161).

■ *Special education and computer chess programs*

Michael David Wojcio (1990) has taught special education students to remember (a) the set up of the board; (b) piece names; (c) piece movement; (d) rules; and (e) the concept of **checkmate**. Wojcio has also taught them to sequence, that is, to put the pawns and pieces correctly on the board at the start of the game. Fine motor skills have also been demonstrated by his students as they move the chess pieces and pawns. They have additionally mastered some basic chess strategies, such as center control, developing one's pieces, and thinking before moving. Some of his students also mastered the **en passant** rule (p. 1).

William Levy taught chess to his self-contained class of "perceptually-impaired learning disabled sixth, seventh, and eighth grade youngsters at the Hopatcong Middle School," New Jersey (Levy, 1986, p. 7). Like Wojcio (1990), Levy taught the fundamentals of the game. Wojcio and Levy also made use of computer chess programs. Wojcio found that "communicationally handicapped" students became more interested in computers after practice with the chess programs. Levy (1986, p. 85) thought computer chess programs gave students chances for success without having to compete directly with other players.

Pairings

Odds

Levy ran a tournament within his special education class. One innovation was that the better players had to give odds to the weaker ones. For example, the top player might remove his **queen** and two **rooks** before playing a much weaker opponent. If the weaker opponent won, the next match featured the top player removing a queen and one rook. This odds system created closer matches among all players. Levy (1986, p. 82) asked his best player to play without his queen and **bishop**. The best player was quite nervous, as the game was then extremely close and hard fought. His opponent was excited to come close to winning, something that wouldn't have been possible without receiving the odds of a queen and bishop. A more detailed explanation of how to decide handicaps based on students' chess strengths is in "Teaching Chess with Handicaps," by IM Larry Kaufman (2001). John Buky, Chicago Public Schools teacher and chess coach (http://www.thechessacademy.org), added that time odds are another handicapping system. Buky (personal communication) wrote, "The spread depends on the difference in playing strength of the 2 players. One possibility is 5 minutes to say 2 minutes (for the stronger player). This still keeps the same pieces on the board, yet makes the game more level and interesting."

Close matches are more likely to lead to flow. Csikszentmihalyi (1996) wrote,

> Playing tennis or chess against a much better opponent leads to frustration; against a much weaker opponent, to boredom. In a really enjoy-

able game, the players are balanced on the fine line between boredom and anxiety. The same is true when work, or a conversation, or a relationship is going well. (p. 111)

Round Robin

A pairing system that allows for close matches is a **round robin** tournament among players similar in ability. In a round robin, everyone plays everyone else. A common format is a "quad," where the top group of four plays a round robin, the next best group of four forms a second round robin tournament, and so on.

Swiss System

In the United States, the Swiss system is more common than the round robin system. In a Swiss system, the first round matches the top half with the bottom half of the field. In many cases, no upsets occur; that is, the top players win their games against their opponents. However, in the second round, the winning players from round one play each other. Those games are closer. Likewise, those who lost in round one play others who lost. The level of the players is thus more evenly matched in round two. In subsequent rounds, players within point groups are paired. Point groups are defined by number of wins (worth one point each), draws (1/2 point each), and losses (zero points each).

Horgan (1992) hypothesized that children's exposure to Swiss system pairings might help them **calibrate**. Horgan found that children who had no formal introduction to probability theory could nevertheless predict the performances of themselves and others, and that this ability then generalized to other domains. Calibration was positively correlated with child chess players' age and rating. Horgan (p. 49) added, "Chess educators have argued that chess improves problem solving, but it may be that lessons about success and failure in chess may be more important than the content of the thinking involved."

Horgan (1992, p. 49) lists the following benefits of calibration, which I paraphrase here:

- Less defensiveness and fewer emotional barriers to learning
- Appropriate attributions for success and failure
- Awareness of when situations control them and when they control situations
- Knowing what one already knows and what one needs to work on
- Time management skills for studying, which can in turn contribute to increased success

Another benefit of pairing unequal opponents is that higher- and lower-rated players gain skills from the encounter. One of my 2005 online students, Leah Burnard, wrote,

One piece of information that has stuck with me through many education classes is that pairing students of different abilities (high/low) can have positive outcomes for both students. The low-ability student has a chance to gain skills from the high-ability player. The high-ability player has the chance to actually explain why his skills assist him/her in winning. The valuable skills that can be derived from chess are not just that of winning. Verbal skills and even tolerance are two skills that can be learned from my above example. The high- and low-ability player can explain their "moves" to each other. In addition, both players learn that everybody is not the same and that it is okay to befriend someone who is a better/poorer player than you.

Chapter 4

SACRIFICE

Chess may help students develop an internal **locus of control**. Believing that one can make a difference is a component of self-sacrificing behavior. For example, Harry Potter's friend Ron was willing to sacrifice himself to save his companions in a "living chess" scene. J. K. Rowling's (1997) *Harry Potter and the Sorcerer's Stone* and other literature with chess themes can meet state curriculum objectives.

Moral Development

"Moral development is fostered through consideration of moral conflicts that arise from the social activities of the class and the wider community" (McNeil, 2006, p. 9). According to Robert Coles (1997, p. 98), a child in the elementary school years wants to know how the world works and what behavior is morally correct. The moral importance of the elementary years was similarly described by Coles' mentors, Anna Freud and Erik Erikson. Coles (1997) wrote that literature and teachers can deeply influence children's moral behavior (p. 31). Moral questions should be discussed during literature class, connecting what children learn from stories to the school curriculum (p. 50). Children bring their own moral and intellectual assumptions to each story or moral scenario (Coles, p. 121). For classroom discussions to be meaningful, students should further personalize the moral lesson, through community service or through writing about its incorporation into their lives (Coles, 1997, p. 183).

One important aspect of morality is being willing to sacrifice for other people. In *The Altruistic Personality: Rescuers of Jews in Nazi Europe*, researchers learned that "rather than regarding themselves as mere pawns, subject to the power of external authorities," rescuers, "in significantly larger percentages than nonrescuers, perceived themselves as actors, capable of making and implementing plans and willing to accept the consequences" (Oliner & Oliner, 1988, p. 177).

Internal Locus of Control

Rescuers scored higher on having an internal locus of control than nonrescuers, as measured by the Internal/External Locus of Control Scale (Gurin, Gurin, & Morrison, 1978). People with an internal locus of control believe that their experiences are largely determined by their skill or efforts. People who have an external locus of control often attribute their experiences to fate, chance, or luck. Internal locus of control may be developed early in life through reasoned explanations (as opposed to harsh, physical punishment) from adults, particularly parents (Oliner & Oliner, 1988, pp. 179–183).

Horgan found that successfully competing in Swiss system chess tournaments helps children make appropriate attributions for success and failure (Horgan, 1992, p. 49; see also Chapter 3 in this book). Likewise, I suspect that chess helps a child develop his or her internal locus of control. In every chess position, the chess player is the actor. International Master Rade Milovanovic, the trainer for the University of Texas at Dallas chess team, noted that chess players think for themselves about whom to help. In a newspaper interview, Rade reflected on his life during the war in Bosnia:

> "Suddenly it's very important who you are, what's your religion. I see people break long friendships with people of another nationality." But he never saw this among chess players. "They supported each other. I think this is because they think independently." He points out the motto of the international chess organization, Federation International des Echecs (FIDE): "Gens Una Sumas" [*sic*; the motto is actually Gens Una Sumus]—Latin for "We are all one people."

> "I know this was true for chess players during the war," Rade says. "I've seen this." (Tarrant, 2000, 6F, 7F)

Chess is a domain where one learns that one's actions have consequences. Moreover, a teacher might illustrate for students the connections between making a difference at the chessboard and making a difference in the world. Several curriculum initiatives with this "making a difference" idea have been piloted under the heading of Chess as a Positive Alternative (Lieberman, 2000, pp. 37–39). Consider also

McNeil's description, cited in Chapter 1, of curricula of social reconstruction and social adaptation.

Chess in Literature

Burt Hochberg (1993) wrote, "Chess, like love, like music, has the power to let us see ourselves" (p. xi). In his anthology *The 64-Square Looking Glass*, "writers spanning many countries and more than a hundred years bring their creativity to bear on the narrative power inherent in chess" (Hochberg, inside cover). Included in Hochberg's anthology is the chess game from Lewis Carroll's (1871/1997) *Through the Looking-Glass*. Either Hochberg's anthology or Carroll's classic is a good place to start exploring the intersection of chess and literature.

Through the Looking-Glass

Through the Looking-Glass can be read on many levels. Lewis Carroll, the pen name of Charles Dodgson, was a mathematician. Dodgson was also the son of a prominent Church of England clergyman. According to A. L. Taylor (1952/1979),

> Chess to Dodgson was something far more than a game. As a mathematician he saw the board like a sheet of graph-paper on which it is possible to represent almost anything, and as a theologian he saw in the two sides a far more powerful means of expressing the opposing factions in Church and University than any he had previously hit upon. (p. 97)

According to Taylor's analysis, dogma is represented by the red queen and the Protestant aspect of the Church is represented by the white queen (p. 144).

On another level of analysis, *Through the Looking-Glass* is the chess dream of a seven-and-a-half-year-old girl. Alice begins as a pawn, with a pawn's limited vision of the chess board. When Alice encounters other chess pieces, she sees them only as long as they are a pawn's move away from her. Otherwise, from Alice's perspective, they vanish "into the air" (Carroll, 1871/1997, p. 182). Alice wants to be a queen. Alice's **promotion** quest is a common theme in chess, namely "**queening** a pawn." The following lesson plan is an adaptation from Root (2001, Spring).

Queening a Pawn

■ *Objectives; problem solving, literary response*

Students will solve a **square of the pawn** chess problem (see also the lesson plan in Chapter 8 entitled "Chess Etiquette and the Square of the Pawn").

Figure 4.1

Chess demonstration board.

Figure 4.2

Tournament quality set and board.

Reading/literary response (TEKS). The student expresses and supports responses to various types of texts. The student is expected to: offer observations, make connections, react, speculate, interpret, and raise questions in response to texts; connect, compare, and contrast ideas, themes, and issues across text (taught in grades 4–8).

Students will listen to excerpts from *Through the Looking-Glass* and then write a story in Carroll's style where they imagine themselves as a chess piece or a chess pawn.

■ *Student population: upper elementary, no chess knowledge*

This 30-minute lesson is appropriate for upper elementary students who have little or no knowledge of chess. The literary exercise at the end of the lesson will extend the lesson time an additional 20 minutes.

■ *Materials*

Chess **demonstration board**, chess boards, and chess sets for the chess portion of the lesson. A demonstration board (Figure 4.1) with a set of pieces and carrying case is available from USCF for $40 (USCF member price) or $50 (nonmember price). A chess set matched with an algebraically labeled chess board (Figure 4.2) and carrying bag costs USCF members $17 and nonmembers $21. Each chess set has 16 pawns (8 white, 8 black), 4 rooks (2 white, 2 black), 4 **knight**s (2 white, 2 black), 4 bishops (2 white, 2 black), 2 queens (1 white, 1 black), and 2 kings (1 white, 1 black).

For the reading and writing portions, excerpts from *Through the Looking-Glass* and paper and pencils (or pens) for students are required.

■ *Procedure*

"Queening a pawn" means that a pawn moves to the other side of the board and becomes a queen. In Carroll's chess story, Alice the pawn begins on the second row and advances to the eighth row to become a queen. What she experiences is made memorable through Carroll's poetic and magical writing. Alice encounters Tweedledee and Tweedledum, Humpty Dumpty, and many other fantastic characters on her way to queening.

Here are some examples of how the characters talk in Carroll's book. Later this class period, you will write your own story. In your story, you will be a chess piece or pawn who, like Alice, meets characters who speak in poetry and wordplay about the strange looking-glass world.

- Tweedledum and Tweedledee recited *The Walrus and the Carpenter.* Perhaps its most famous stanza is

"The time has come," the Walrus said,

"To talk of many things:

Of shoes—and ships—and sealing-wax—

Of cabbages—and kings—

And why the sea is boiling hot—

And whether pigs have wings." (p. 203)

- The White Queen remarked,

"The rule is, jam to-morrow and jam yesterday—but never jam to-day."
"It *must* come sometimes to 'jam to-day,'" Alice objected.
"No, it can't," said the Queen. "It's jam every *other* day: to-day isn't any *other* day, you know." (Carroll, p. 216, italics in the original)

- Humpty Dumpty informed Alice that

"There are three hundred and sixty-four days when you might get un-birthday presents—"

"Certainly," said Alice.

"And only *one* for birthday presents, you know. There's glory for you!"

"I don't know what you mean by 'glory,'" Alice said.

Humpty Dumpty smiled contemptuously. "Of course you don't—till I tell you. I meant 'there's a nice knock-down argument for you!'"

"But 'glory' doesn't mean 'a nice knock-down argument,'" Alice objected.

"When *I* use a word," Humpty Dumpty said in rather a scornful tone, "it means just what I choose it to mean—neither more nor less." (Carroll, p. 237, italics in the original)

With her limited vision and her height of less than three inches, Alice hesitated at the entrance to a dark wood. "However, on second thoughts, she made up her mind to go on: 'for I certainly won't go *back*,' she thought to herself, and this was the only way to the Eighth Square" (Carroll, 1871/1997, p. 193, italics in original). In the **chess diagram** shown in Figure 4.3, our lone pawn is on the square e2.

Chess Diagram: Alice chess problem

Black to move

Figure 4.3

The teacher should show the diagrammed position on a chess demonstration board and say,

We can tell the square's name, e2, by checking first the **file**, or vertical name, e, and then the **rank**, or horizontal name, 2. Imagine that Alice is the white pawn. If she can make it to e8 without being captured, she will become a white queen. In our chess lesson Alice will be chased by the enemy king. The enemy king is on the square a4. The enemy king has a head start because black will move first from the diagrammed position.

Do you think the enemy king can catch Alice? That question is the subject of our chess lesson, and to answer it we need chess rules. Lewis Carroll did not follow real chess rules in *Through the Looking-Glass*. For example, Carroll let the white side make 13 moves and the black side only 3.

For our chess lesson, we will follow the real chess rules. After the black king moves, it is Alice's turn to move. A pawn can jump one or two squares straight forward on her first move. After a pawn's first move, she moves one square forward at a time. The king can move one square at a time in any direction. The king captures by moving onto the same square as an enemy piece—such as a pawn in our case—and removing that enemy.

Now that we know the rules for Alice and the black king, let's see what might happen for each of them during our chess lesson. We will count before we actually move the pieces and pawns. In the chess diagram, the black king could go to a3, a5, b3, b4, or b5. Black's goal is to stop Alice from becoming a queen, so he will probably head for her promotion square: e8. One path to e8 is along the a-file and then along the 8th rank. How many moves would that take?

Give students a chance to think, and then show that the answer is 8: a5, a6, a7, a8, b8, c8, d8, and e8.

What happens if the king moves along a diagonal to e8? Black makes 4 moves in this case: b5, c6, d7, e8. What square should Alice choose for her first move: e3 or e4? It seems like the best chance to queen is to run quickly toward the promotion square. Alice's total moves to queen are 5: e4, e5, e6, e7, e8. Do you think the enemy king can catch Alice? Yes! The black king moving along the diagonal will capture Alice in four moves, since Alice will take five moves to queen.

To check this answer, set up a chessboard and play out the moves.

■ *Practice*

Partner students up, and give each pair a chessboard, a black king, and a white pawn. Have them set up the chess diagram position with black to move. After each partner has had a chance to practice with the black king, tell them to change the problem. Have it be white's move from the initial position. See if Alice the pawn gets to queen (without being captured) if she moves first. The answer should still be "no."

■ *Literary exercise*

After students pack up the chess boards, ask them to imagine themselves as the pawn in the exercise. If some students know chess, they can imagine themselves as a piece instead. Ask each student to write about moving as a pawn, what happens when he or she encounters enemy chessmen, and what things chess pawns and pieces might say. Tell students they can use the Carroll quotes as inspiration for their writing.

Like Alice, Harry Potter is a young person set on achieving a goal in a world filled with strange happenings and powerful figures. In Harry's case, the world is Hogwarts, a school for wizards and witches.

Harry Potter and the Sorcerer's Stone

In one scene of *Harry Potter and the Sorcerer's Stone*, by J. K. Rowling (1997), Harry and his friends Ron and Hermione must cross a room with gigantic chess pieces. The chess game is one step in the ongoing struggle to defeat the evil Voldemort, killer of Harry's parents. Hermione, Ron, and Harry assume the positions of a black rook, knight, and bishop. Ron directs the play of all the black forces, as he is the best chess player. Each time a black piece is taken, it is horribly beaten and dragged unconscious to the side of the board.

In contrast to Carroll's detailed chess score, not many moves are given in the Rowling chess scene. Rowling refers to Harry moving four squares to the right, to Hermione taking a bishop, to threats narrowly avoided by Harry and Hermione, and to the captures of black chessmen. Lewis Carroll used a system called descriptive notation, where one writes of, for example, the king's pawn moving to king's four. Nowadays, algebraic notation is more common (see Chapter 8, "Notation Lesson for the Future," for an explanation of algebraic notation and the glossary for a definition of the term *notation*).

Rowling used no chess notation, but International Master Jeremy Silman (2002) imagined a game score for her words. His ideas were used in the movie *Harry Potter and the Sorcerer's Stone*. In the Harry Potter chess scene, Ron realizes that he must be taken in order to win the game. He has to decide whether to sacrifice himself so that his classmate Harry can checkmate the enemy king. Ron's sacrifice would allow Harry to continue his quest for the sorcerer's stone (Rowling, 1997, p. 283). I won't give away the ending of this living chess scene, but reading an excerpt about Ron's intended sacrifice could spark moral discussion among your students. Also possible is a chess exercise, such as the one that follows, where students read the Potter chess passage and then, like Silman, create their own game score to accompany Rowling's words.

Plotting Potter's Pieces

■ *Objectives; literary analysis TEKS, writing in a genre, chess creativity*

Reading/text structures/literary concepts (TEKS). The student analyzes the characteristics of various types of texts (genres). The student is expected to: identify the purposes of different types of texts, such as to inform, influence, express, or entertain; recognize and analyze story plot, setting, and problem resolution (taught in grades 4–8).

In this lesson, students will have a choice of writing in an informative style or creating a chess score sheet (or series of diagrams) that conveys what happened in the Harry Potter chess game.

■ *Student population: upper elementary, intermediate chess knowledge*

This two-period (two 50-minute class times) chess and literature lesson is appropriate for upper elementary and middle school students who have learned how chess pieces and pawns move and know what checkmate is. Additionally, students should be able to read and write chess notation and know how to create chess diagrams. See Chapter 8 for lessons that teach these skills.

■ *Materials*

For the first 50-minute class period: chess demonstration board, chess boards, chess pieces and pawns, score sheets, blank chess diagrams; excerpt (pp. 281–284) from *Harry Potter and the Sorcerer's Stone*; and paper and pencils (or pens) for students. Ideally (in addition to the materials for class period one), computers, chess software for making diagrams, and printers should be available for the second 50-minute class period.

■ *Procedure*

Have the students read silently the chess scene from *Harry Potter and the Sorcerer's Stone* (pp. 281–284 in the Scholastic paperback edition of the book). Discuss with the class the setting of the scene: chessboard, chamber, living pieces. Discuss the problem in the scene: Harry must get across the chamber, but can't until he wins the chess game. Optional: If students have been reading this book, discuss how this scene fits into the plot.

Ask how the scene could be converted from story-telling style into an information bulletin, for example a report for the wizard's newspaper the *Daily Prophet*. Note that the scene could also be viewed as a chess game. Show the game from the Silman (2002) Web site on the chess demonstration board.

Then give students a choice of what they would like to work on: a newspaper report on what happened to the chess pieces (including

Harry, Ron, and Hermione), or creating a game score for what moves were played. Form groups of three or four students to begin the projects. Allow groups to work on their projects for the rest of the 50-minute period.

■ *Chess practice*

For the groups that chose creating a game score, give them a printout of the chess game from Silman's (2002) Web site to use as a model for their work. Let them have chess pieces and pawns, a chess board, score sheets, blank chess diagrams, pencils, and paper to record their ideas in notation. Tell them that they don't have to start from move one. That is, they could just create a chess problem position where one piece is sacrificed and then develop two or three more diagrams to show what happens when the sacrifice is accepted.

■ *Literary exercise*

For students who are working on the newspaper report of the incident, have them reread the excerpt. Tell them to pretend they are reporters from the *Daily Prophet*, the newspaper for the wizard world. In other words, they are to view the scene as having actually happened. Remind them to put "who, what, where, when, and why" in the first paragraph of their newspaper report of the chess game.

■ *Conclusion*

During the second 50-minute period allow time for students to finish their work in groups using paper and pencil. Then move to a computer lab. Allow students to type and to publish (print) their newspaper reports and to use chess software (if available) to make professional-looking chess diagrams. Each literary-group student could be responsible for typing up a different page of the newspaper report, or for making art to illustrate the news story. With the chess groups, students could each make a different diagram of what they've created and then serve as proofreaders for each others' work. If chess software is not available, have the students type the notation. Alternatively, students could use their handwritten notes to show the class on the demonstration board what they have created.

Reading List

With your instruction, chess scenes from Carroll, Rowling, and other authors may serve state-mandated objectives. The TEKS cited in the lesson plans for *Queening a Pawn* and *Plotting Potter's Pieces* demonstrate how chess-themed literature might enhance your curriculum. Appendix A lists objectives similar to these TEKS taken from other states' standards.

Other literary works for preschool to grade 8 that include chess themes are listed in the following bulleted list. Further information is available at Amazon.com, which (along with personal knowledge) was my source for publication information and plot descriptions. In alphabetical order, by author's last name:

- Bailey, Len. (2005). *Clabbernappers*. Starscape. Ages 9–12. A junior rodeo champion opens an amusement park door and enters a checkerboard world of fantastic characters, including chess pieces.
- Birch, David. (1993, reprint). *The King's Chessboard*. Puffin. Ages 4–8. Story based on the mathematics of chess: How many grains of rice are used if one places one on the first chess square, two on the second, four on the third, and then continue to double the rice grains until the 64th square?
- Farber, Erica. (1996). *Kiss of the Mermaid (Step into Reading, Step 3, paper)*. Random House Books for Young Readers. Ages 4–8. When Pooka turns all of the merpeople into stone, Thistle hopes to secure their release by winning a chess game against the evil sea witch.
- Garrow, Simon. (1983). *The Amazing Adventure of Dan the Pawn*. Simon & Schuster. Ages 4–8. Dan, an inexperienced pawn, learns the names and movements of the different chess pieces and pawns, and takes part in an attack on the enemy king. There is an end section that includes rules for playing chess.
- Harper, Piers. (2001). *Checkmate at Chess City*. Walker. Ages 7–10. Using the moves of individual chessmen, the reader helps the black pawns, knights, bishops, and rooks move through a series of maze-like scenes to enter Chess City and free their king and queen.
- Keene, Carolyn. (1999, reprint). *The Case of the Captured Queen: Nancy Drew #147*. Aladdin. Ages 9–12. Greta must win if she wants to see her sister alive again, and as the tournament progresses, the tension builds. The kidnapper is a grand master of menace and deception, and it's up to Nancy to make all the right moves in this deadly game.
- Kraus, Robert. (2000). *Mort the Sport*. Scholastic. Ages 4–8. Mort plays many sports, but when his parents ask him what he'd like to try next he says chess—because he wants to sit down.
- Kusen, Michael. (2000). *Chess Poems*. Tandem (available at http://www.chesshouse.com/). Ages 4–10. These light-hearted poems are instructionally accurate to the basic concepts of the game, and their blend of rhyming humor and fantasy make them a joy for any child.
- Levy, Elizabeth. (1983). *The Computer That Said Steal Me*. Four Winds. Ages 9–12. A sixth grader's consuming desire for a computer chess game leads him into serious trouble.
- Levy, Elizabeth. (2002). *Vampire State Building*. HarperCollins. Ages 9–12. Computer chess and chat between a New York boy and a Romanian boy develops into a vampire mystery.

- Mahony, Mary. *Stand Tall, Harry*. Redding. Ages 9–13. Harry is an African American student who is bused from the city to the suburbs for his education. Harry shares with his grandfather his desire to find a best friend at his new school. Eventually, Harry befriends a boy named Jack, and their friendship ultimately brings them both to the chessboard. Harry endures a serious hockey injury, an eventual diagnosis of scoliosis, and soon finds himself as a possible U.S. chess star.
- Robinson, Nancy K. (1994). *Countess Veronica*. Scholastic Trade. Ages 9–12. Veronica encourages her mother's romance with a chess grandmaster
- Shura, Mary. (1986). *The Josie Gambit*. New York: Dodd, Mead. Ages 9–12. Shy, 12-year-old, chess-loving Greg is apprehensive about spending six months with his grandmother in Pineville, Illinois; but his relationship with the outgoing Nolan family involves him in some real-life chess moves with a troubled girl that open him up to loyalty and friendship with people who really count.
- Sutcliff, Rosemary. (1993). *Chess-Dream in the Garden*. Walker. Ages 4–8. A picture book that features the story of the discovery of the Isle of Lewis chess pieces
- Tan, Amy. 1990. *The Joy Luck Club*. Ivy. Kathy Lancaster, Hedrick (Lewisville ISD, TX) middle school librarian, suggested a lesson plan based on the chapter "Waverly Jong: The Rules of the Game." Waverly, girl chess champion, feels that her mother lives vicariously through Waverly's victories. Lancaster suggested that middle school students read the chapter and then discuss how parental expectations affect them.
- Waitzkin, Fred. (1990). *Searching for Bobby Fischer*. Penguin. Ages 10–adult. The father of a chess prodigy observes the world of chess. This title also became an Academy Award–nominated film.
- Wong, Janet S. (2004). *Alex and the Wednesday Chess Club*. Margaret K. McElderry. Ages 4–8. Four-year-old Alex loses at chess to an adult and gives up the game for sports. In third grade, he rekindles his interest in chess and finds new chess pals at the Wednesday afternoon chess club.

Teachers might include some of the above titles in their classroom reading collection. School and public librarians might consider a chess-themed book display or developing a library chess program. Libraries often have long, rectangular tables perfectly sized for chess boards. Additionally, a library can accommodate a bigger chess program than can an individual teacher's classroom. Libraries are excellent locations for chess clubs, according to Sullivan (2003). Boys' reading test scores are a year and a half behind those of girls, and boys are less likely to visit libraries (Sullivan, 2003). Many boys believe "the stereotype that reading and other intellectual pursuits are passive and effeminate" (Sullivan, 2003, p. 58). Chess draws boys into libraries and "also has a humanizing effect for library staff members. Like police playing midnight basketball with at-risk teens, a library chess program creates an avenue of exposure for the library, welcoming children and families into a fun atmosphere, cementing a relationship before the library's other services are needed" (Sullivan, 2003, p. 60). Sullivan lists specific steps for developing library chess programs, complementing the recommendations for the development of school chess programs made by Barber (2003).

Chapter 5

PROBLEM SOLVING

One of the great debates in psychology and education is which comes first, content or thinking? In other words, is thinking tied to specific content areas, or are there general problem-solving heuristics? Two opposing views from chess psychological research, those of William Chase and de Groot, are presented. Problem-solving heuristics from de Groot, the TEKS, and George Polya (mathematics) are nearly identical. Heuristics from Merrill Harmin (moral education) and Csikszentmihalyi (surviving desperate circumstances) are analogous to de Groot's chess-based problem-solving heuristic. In the second half of this chapter, two leading chess coaches' approaches are presented.

Content or General Heuristics?

De Groot's Chess Player Experiments

De Groot's work helped lay the foundation for the cognitive science revolution of the 1960s (Gobet, 1999, p. 84). De Groot collected data from several rating levels of chess players, including the top players of the late 1930s. De Groot asked his subjects to verbalize their thoughts about their prospective next move in an unfamiliar chess position (Gobet, 1999, p. 87). From this qualitative interview data, de Groot found that thought processes are similar among all chess players. That is, players similarly verbalized, "If I move here, he'll move there. And

I'll like that resulting position." Chess players' verbal protocols represent general problem-solving heuristics. Such heuristics do not, however, explain **expertise**, or distinguish the chess master from the chess amateur (Chase & Simon, 1973).

Decision Process in Chess

The decision process in chess "characterizes most complex, goal-directed thought and choice processes, scientific activity included." (Gobet, 1999, p. 89). For that reason, the decision process should be taught to school children. De Groot, in his 1977 memorandum, wrote,

> As a matter of course, general heuristics—general problem solving methods—being "general," can be learned by means of many types of subject matter, all traditional school subjects included. Does not this make chess instruction superfluous?
>
> For an answer to this question three points must be emphasized. First, general heuristics tend to take root only if their being learned is stimulated and promoted in more than one subject context. Therefore, in this respect chess instruction can be a fruitful, unorthodox *addition* to the learning environment. Second, *some* of the learning effects mentioned above, *are specific*—not to chess, but—to learning by doing, in situations where the pupil himself can (learn to) take rational decisions, on his own responsibility. *Games* like chess—being "playful," requiring personal decisions, and producing naturally short-cycle feedback information for learning—opponent's moves—would appear to provide *the best possible learning environment. . . .* Third, it is quite true that other games such as checkers and go [a Chinese board game], if taught in school, could serve this particular purpose as well as chess. (de Groot, 1981, p. 8, emphasis in the original)

Nevertheless, de Groot recommended chess to educators because of its cultural legacy and international popularity. De Groot's second point, that learning in chess comes from playing, may depend on the style of the chess instructor. This issue will be further discussed in the second half of this chapter, where teacher-directed and constructivist instructional styles are compared.

■ *Compared to decision process in other domains*

De Groot's first point—that through exposure to problem solving in more than one subject matter, general heuristics will be more likely to be learned by pupils—is explored by analogy in the next few paragraphs. General heuristics, like those described by de Groot, are also found in the TEKS, Polya (mathematics), Harmin (moral education), and Csikszentmihalyi (surviving desperate circumstances).

As described by Gobet, de Groot's "four phases of chess thought" correspond to the TEKS problem-solving heuristic for mathematics and Polya's (1957) *How to Solve It*. All table entries in Figure 5.1 are from

Figure 5.1

Problem-solving heuristics.

Gobet (1999, p. 89)	TEKS Mathematics	Polya (1957, pp. xvi–xvii)
Orientation	Understanding the problem	Understanding the problem
Exploration	Making a plan	Devising a plan
Investigation	Carrying out the plan	Carrying out the plan
Proof	Evaluating the solution for reasonableness	Looking back

those three sources. For mathematics standards from other states that are similar to the TEKS, see Appendix A.

One educator's description of the type of intelligence needed for moral behavior is comparable to the problem-solving heuristic:

> We want students to stop and think, to be aware, to remember what they have learned, to look ahead, to weigh alternatives before acting, and to appreciate the wisdom of those who have gone before them. (Harmin, 1990, p. 8)

Similar also are the steps that Csikszentmihalyi summarized from Richard Logan's study of survivors:

> First, they paid close attention to the most minute details of their environment, discovering in it hidden opportunities for action that matched what little they were capable of doing, given the circumstances. Then they set goals appropriate to their precarious situation, and closely monitored progress through the feedback they received. Whenever they reached their goal, they upped the ante, setting increasingly complex challenges for themselves. (Csikszentmihalyi, 1990, p. 90)

Having identified possible similarities between problem solving in chess and in other domains, we can now examine how chess is taught in U.S. schools.

Teacher Directed or Constructivist?

De Groot (1981) characterized, then responded to, the question of transfer from chess to other objectives as follows:

> It may be true that chessplayers have learned some tricks of rational "future thinking," but then they tend to practice them solely on the chessboard. . . . How is it possible to promote such transfer, by organizing teaching and learning in one field in such a way that the "transferability" of potentially more general learning effects to other fields of activity is maximized? I am not suggesting that the latter problem is a simple one. But I am suggesting that it is an educational task to try

and solve it. As regards the teaching of chess, it must be possible to do this in such a way—and along with the teaching of other subjects—that its game-, decision-, planning- and future-related learning effects become less "specific" and more transferable than they appear to be if chess is learnt outside the educational context. (pp. 8–9)

Two different ways of presenting chess to students are exemplified by Sunil Weeramantry and Stephen Shutt.

Direct Instruction for Chess Mastery: Sunil Weeramantry

At the USCF's Chess in Education workshop (St. Paul, 2000), master chess coach Weeramantry, stepfather of 2000 National Elementary Champion H. Nakamura, described his chess training technique. His students don't have sets and boards in front of them during lecture time: Eyes are on Weeramantry's chess demonstration board. Weeramantry has developed a technological, teacher-directed program of chess training. He presents series of problems on the demonstration board. Intuitive, called-out answers are discouraged. Whether individually slow or fast at chess, students analyze together according to principles of chess (such as **pins**, **forks**, and king position) that Weeramantry has outlined. Students then practice chess problems according to the same principles while Weeramantry monitors their work.

Weeramantry believes that students who attempt to play chess without approximately 40 hours of direct instruction in chess principles do not know how to think. They are paralyzed by lack of chess knowledge, thus sit unable to make chess moves. Weeramantry considers chess a subject matter worthy of serious study. He thinks that there are correct ways to play chess—ways that students learn most efficiently by his methods. Weeramantry said he likes to be in control of his students and their chess development.

■ *Cultural literacy history teaching*

Weeramantry's view of chess reminds me of the cultural literacy style of school history teaching. Cultural literacy historians want students to establish a firm foundation of facts and patriotism before being exposed to the complexity of historical interpretations: "In other words, facts first, interpretations (much) later" (Root, 1999, p. 2). I characterized one teacher I studied for my dissertation as being from the cultural literacy school of history, because she preferred lectures and outlines of history. Student talk was infrequent, and commonly took the form of recitation. Her students "accepted the job of learning more history facts to prepare for the Advanced Placement examination" (Root, 1999, p. 107).

Piagetian Chess for Discovery: Stephen Shutt

Stephen Shutt, the coach of the national champion Masterman High School team, presented immediately after Weeramantry at the Chess in Education workshop. Shutt has students "discover" the rules of chess. For example, he will move a rook around the board and encourage his student to do the same. Through experimentation, the student deduces how the rook moves. Shutt terms his approach "Piagetian," in that students construct their own understandings of the rules and principles of chess.

After individualized rules practice (coach with each student one-on-one), Shutt lets each student have a chess board and time to handle the chess pieces. Shutt allows students to play against one another, learning by doing. Shutt considers himself as a support system rather than as an authority figure for his chess players.

■ *New history dialogic teaching*

Shutt's approach is analogous to the "New History" theory of school history instruction: "The New History perspective, history intertwined with Self, leads students to examine and create alternate historical interpretations. . . . Teachers pursuing New History ideals may adopt more interchanges of thought, or *dialogic* discourse" (Root, 1999, p. 4, italics in original). The dialogic teacher I studied for my dissertation encouraged her students to present their own interpretations of 1960s U.S. history. Miss Madison's characterizations of history were springboards for students' thoughts:

> For example, her characterization of the Vietnam era as the beginning of people questioning authority intrigued students. Several students felt that not everyone questioned authority today, that Miss Madison was wrong about Vietnam and its impact. Ironically, their questioning of her interpretation supports its thrust. (Root, p. 108)

If there are commonalities across disciplines in terms of general heuristics, how are those connections best made by students and teachers? Does it make a difference if the lessons are teacher-directed or constructivist? And what about the issue of transfer; that is, if one learns heuristics in chess will one apply them in other situations? These are questions that remain critical for the future of chess in the schools. As more teachers include chess in their classrooms, the efficacy of transfer will be a fruitful topic for classroom research by teachers themselves or by educational researchers.

Chapter 6

MULTIPLE INTELLIGENCES (MI)

In this chapter the nature of expertise is explored. What makes an expert different from an amateur? Pattern recognition turns out to be critical. And, in chess, patterns are detected visuospatially. Because chess taps spatial intelligence, chess is an alternative instructional method for developing students' knowledge of scholastic domains. Gardner's theory proposes that multiple intelligences (MI) be used to teach domains. According to Gardner, most classroom activities rely primarily on linguistic and logical mathematical intelligences, so spatial intelligence activities such as chess provide a valuable contrast to pencil and paper seatwork. Chess may activate bodily kinesthetic intelligence by the small motor movements used to move chess pieces or by the large motor movements necessary to act out a game (living chess).

Expertise

Experts perceive meaningful patterns in their domains, solve problems quickly with little error, have superior short-term and long-term memory, see and represent problems in their domain at a deeper (more principled) level than novices, qualitatively analyze problems, and have strong self-monitoring skills (paraphrased from Chi, Glaser, and Farr, 1988, pp. xvii–xx).

Studies of chess have been instrumental in forming cognitive scientists' view of expertise. Cited in many texts is de Groot's research of the late 1930s to 1940s, published in English (1966) as "Perception and Memory Versus Thought: Some Old Ideas and Recent Findings." De Groot found that chess masters recalled glimpsed chess positions more accurately than chess novices. This finding held true as long as the position was from a real game. If the pieces were randomly arranged, masters and novices remembered similarly small numbers of pieces. De Groot's results suggest that knowledge of a domain (e.g., chess) is more important in expertise than a generally good memory.

Pattern Recognition

Expanding on de Groot's research, Chase and Simon (1973, p. 217) found that pattern recognition is one of the most important processes for chess skill. When confronted with unfamiliar positions, and asked to recall them, masters tended to remember chunks of information. Those chunks had structures important to chess functions, such as a **castle**d king's position or one piece defending another one. At the same time, chess functional structures are built around visual features such as **pawn chain**s, piece clusters, piece color, and spatial location of pieces (Chase & Simon, 1973, pp. 232–233); see Figure 6.1.

The Mind's Eye

According to Chase and Simon (1973), thinking in chess takes place in the **mind's eye.** The mind's eye "is the meeting point where visual information from the external world is combined and coordinated with visual representations stored in short-term and long-term memory" (p. 277). Chase and Simon found that, when a master looks at the chess board, he sees smaller clusters of pieces. Those clusters often have moves associated with them in long-term memory. Therefore, the master begins his search for his next move by using moves from his memory bank and analyzing what would happen if he tried that move in his current game (p. 269). Having decided on a likely move, the master looks at the board, focusing on the spot where the piece would be after his imagined move. He then forms an image of the generated move with the pieces already physically in place on the board (Chase & Simon, p. 270).

This use of visual cues explains why blindfold chess is challenging. In blindfold chess, no verification of the external board position is possible (Chase & Simon, 1973, p. 277). For regular chess games, "peripheral vision is important because the fovea can resolve only a very few squares (perhaps 4)" (Chase & Simon, p. 270). Peripheral vision signals where the few squares seen by the fovea are in relation to the rest of the 64-square chess board. Visual information from the fovea and from peripheral vision allows the chess player to update the chess position previously stored in his mind's eye. A similar phenomenon occurs when a driver approaches a traffic light at a familiar inter-

Figure 6.1

Kingside castled positions with pawn chains.

section. Although her fovea focuses on the red, yellow, or green of the traffic light, the driver's peripheral vision takes in the intersecting streets and adjacent sidewalks. Her peripheral vision thus allows a relatively complete picture of the intersection to form in her mind's eye. Imagine how much harder it would be for her to drive if she were only told that the light was red, yellow, or green, without being permitted to visually check the rest of her surroundings. Blindfold chess players are told the move currently being made (the "red, yellow, or green" in our traffic example), but they can't refresh their vision of the entire chess board. Chase and Simon's findings generated further research on the topics of chess, expertise, perception, and memory. It would be impossible to summarize the academic work here. One refinement, by Gobet & Simon (1996), is the recognition of long-term memory retrieval structures. Those "templates specify the locations of perhaps a dozen pieces in the position (thus specifying a class of positions), but also contain variables (slots) in which additional information can be placed, thus fixing the positions of additional pieces" (p. 29). Despite this theoretical modification, chunks and visual-spatial features are still vibrant, important constructs. Other researchers agree that "pattern recognition processes underlie superior performance by skilled chess players" (Schultetus & Charness, 1999, p. 555; this article includes a comprehensive bibliography on the topics).

Spatial Intelligence

The perceptual skills utilized by chess players appear in other domains. Painters visualize what their painting will look like with additional brush strokes. Sculptors think about how a planned next cut will influence form. These spatial skills are "operations that have been shown experimentally to be performable" in the mind's eye (Chase & Simon, 1973, p. 271). Likewise, as illustrated in Figure 6.2,

> People seem to solve problems of the form *If A is better than B, and C is worse than B, then who is best?* by placing A, B, and C in a mental image and replacing *better* by the spatial relation *above*. Then to find *best* or *worst*, people find the top or bottom item, respectively, in the image. People seem to solve these problems faster by this "spatial paralogic" than by the use of deductive reasoning. (Chase & Simon, p. 272; italics in the original)

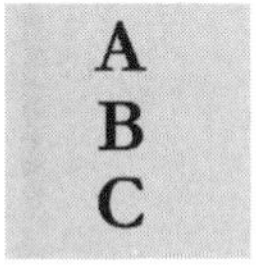

A
B
C

Figure 6.2

Spatial paralogic: Problem-solving in the mind's eye.

Chess and Reading Comprehension

Using the mind's eye to play chess may strengthen students' "spatial paralogic" abilities, which they use to solve some reading comprehension problems. For example, Margulies (1996) found that third- and fourth-grade classes that received chess and general reasoning instruction outscored their matched counterparts on a reading post-test. In each of the five schools studied, reading pre-test scores showed no significant differences between the classes about to receive chess instruction and the control group classes, which would receive basic skills instruction from their classroom teachers. After 24 to 48 hours of either chess or basic skills instruction, students in the chess group and the control group took a reading post-test.

A question from the post-test used by Margulies (1996) asked students to compare four people by weight after reading a narrative text that gave their names, some extraneous information, and their weights. Spatial paralogic in the mind's eye would help children solve this reading comprehension problem, as the weights could be ranked from heaviest to lightest. Improved spatial paralogic might account for the consistently better post-test reading scores of the chess group versus the control group in Margulies's study.

State Reading Standards

Learning spatial paralogic equips students with an important strategy for understanding text, meeting the following grades 4–8 TEKS objective (http://www.tea.state.tx.us): "Reading/comprehension. The student comprehends selections using a variety of strategies."

For similar reading standards from other states, see Appendix A.

Figure 6.3
Stacked chess pieces.

Bodily Kinesthetic Intelligence

Bodily kinesthetic intelligence can be activated by chess. Besides practicing the chess moves on a chessboard, consider having your students become the pieces and move around a room. When my daughter was younger, she used to move diagonally across our tiled kitchen floor. She stated, "I'm moving like a bishop now." Her action was a mini-version of a living chess game. In living chess games, costumed participants move like pieces following the directions of the game score sheet.

The smaller body movements of touching, holding, and moving pieces also appeal to kinesthetic learners. Many young chess players enjoy building towers out of captured pieces (Figure 6.3) or creating a distinctive style of moving a piece (e.g., sliding it across the squares, or bringing it down with a bang).

The **touch move** rule states that if you touch a piece you have to move it, and if you let go of the piece the move is final. During the learning stage, as students struggle to visualize the results of their planned next moves, consider suspending the touch move rule. Chess may be more understandable to some learners if they physically complete, THEN contemplate, each move.

Chapter 7

PLANNING

Students learn life-planning skills through chess. The larger lessons that chess offers are contemplated in this chapter through references to the humanistic curriculum, chess books, and anecdotes. Chess problems and positions illustrate themes within the self-directed curriculum. A summary of research on games as part of a lifetime mental health plan ends the chapter.

The Self-Directed Curriculum

One branch of humanistic curriculum is the self-directed curriculum: "Humanists believe that the basics should include a sense of ability, clarity of values, positive self-concept, capacity for innovation, and openness—characteristics of the self-directed learner" (McNeil, 2006, pp. 8–9). The self-directed curriculum plans for development along five fronts: *Cognitive, Affective, Social, Moral,* and *Ego Development.* This chapter contains McNeil's descriptions of the development aims of four of the fronts, supplemented with chess examples. (Moral development was considered in Chapter 4.)

Cognitive

Cognitive. Children respond to the requirements of problematic situations, not simply to external directions. By anticipating consequences, they learn to make wise choices about goals. (McNeil, 2006, p. 9)

Once students learn the rules of chess, self-directed learning is the nature of the game. Each game presents problems never before encountered by the student. Through practice, students' choices become wiser.

Ben Franklin thought chess players might learn "*Foresight*, which looks a little into futurity, and considers the Consequences that may attend an action; for it is continually occurring to the Player, 'If I move this piece, what will be the advantages or disadvantages of my new situation? What Use can my Adversary make of it to annoy me? What other moves can I make to support it, and to defend myself from his attacks?'" (Franklin, B., 1779/1987, p. 928, italics in original).

School counselors often work with young people who lack good decision-making skills. Some students neglect homework, some disregard classroom rules, and some succumb to peer pressure to try drugs, sex, or criminal activity. Others may come from dysfunctional or abusive homes. Fernando Moreno (2002) used chess as part of his school counseling work with K–12 students. One premise of his work is that chess can be seen as an analogy to life. In chess we control our own pieces, but we don't control our opponent's moves. Similarly, in life, we control our own decisions and choices. But the environment (the actions of parents, other adults, and peers) is not in our control. Therefore, we must choose the best moves in our particular situation. If someone suggests a move to us, we should think rather than blindly following the advice.

Moreno (2002) uses chess games to drive home his points. For example, he might purposefully suggest a bad move to a team of students playing another team of students. When the first team follows Moreno's advice and loses a piece or pawn, Moreno reminds the team members that they are responsible for their choices. Making the connection to life, he adds, "*Sometimes older people can make suggestions to do things, but you have to be alert and decide if they are good choices to follow*" (pp. 32–33, italics in original). The next time Moreno makes a suggestion, team members think before accepting or rejecting his advice. Moreno reinforces their thoughtfulness by saying, "*You can make good decisions, you can do the same in your life/school*" (p. 33, italics in original).

Affective

> *Affective*. Children learn to deal at an emotional level with such uncertainties as social conflicts, evaluation, and challenge. They learn to view failure as a learning experience. (McNeil, 2006, p. 9)

Ben Franklin wrote that chess taught perseverance:

We learn by Chess the habit of not being discouraged by present appearances in the state of our affairs, the habit of hoping for a favourable Change, and that of persevering in the search of resources. The Game is so full of Events, there is such a variety of turns in it, the Fortune of it is so subject to sudden Vicissitudes, and one so frequently, after long contemplation, discovers the means of extricating one's self from a supposed insurmountable Difficulty, that one is encouraged to continue the Contest to the last. (Franklin, B., 1779/1987, p. 929)

Similarly, Csikszentmihalyi (1990) wrote,

The integrity of the self depends on the ability to take neutral or destructive events and turn them into positive ones. . . . It is for this reason that courage, resilience, perseverance, mature defense, or transformational coping—the dissipative structures of the mind—are so essential. Without them we would be constantly suffering through the random bombardment of stray psychological meteorites. On the other hand, if we do develop such positive strategies, most negative events can be at least neutralized, and possibly even used as challenges that will help make the self stronger and more complex. (p. 202)

Social

Social. Assertiveness training, role training, and experimenting with competitive and cooperative groups are among the activities provided. (McNeil, 2006, p. 9)

Chess provides opportunities to meet new people. A parent of a six-year-old girl reports, "She's blossomed from [chess competition]. . . . It takes a lot of moxie to sit down and play against someone you don't know and match wits with them" (Hucks, 1999, p. B6). When children practice chess together, positive cooperative interactions occur. School counselor Forest Rosser (Pleasant Valley Elementary, Oregon) said, "It's great to see the more experienced players mentor the ones who are eager to learn the game" (Thomas, 1999, p. C3).

Moreno (2002) used chess with bilingual and ESOL (English Speakers of Other Languages) students. Moreno believes that chess shows students that people's minds work in similar ways. Also, the game provides a nonlanguage format for interacting with people of diverse cultures. These aspects of chess highlight our common humanity. On the other hand, the pieces of chess are different (just like students), and each piece has its own strengths and weaknesses (again, just like students). Thus, chess also shows the diversity of humankind. Finally, chess was a non-threatening way for Moreno to open interactions with new students. Sometimes new students are reluctant to talk about their problems with a counselor. Playing a game is a way to build a relationship until talking becomes more comfortable.

Ego Development

> *Ego development.* The development of self-respect and self-confidence occurs through a social climate in which a person's world does not depend on ability or level of maturity. Each individual has an opportunity to attain success for there is no scarcity of rewards. (McNeil, 2006, p. 9)

Undergraduates with no knowledge of chess can learn the rules in about 20 minutes (Yoskowitz, 1991, p. 359). Knowledge of English is not required. Chess can be played by young and old, by rich and poor, and by gifted and special needs children:

> Chess is one of the few fields in which some children become true prodigies. . . . Ollie LaFreniere, a retired Shoreline District chess coach who led teams to five state titles in the 1980s . . . [says], "I try to warn the big kids to be very careful about the size of the opponent across the board." Chess, the great equalizer. (Ramirez, 1992, p. 16)

In an interview, Bruce Pandolfini said,

> Playing chess gives us a chance to start our life over again, and this time no one has more money than us, no one is more beautiful, no one lives in a better neighborhood, and we all go to the same school. Other than having the first move, and this benefit is shared equally, no one starts with any unfair advantage. (Killigrew, 2000b, p. 39)

Figure 7.1 shows the starting position of a chess game, with equal numbers of pieces and pawns for each side. White moves first in chess.

Chess as Lifelong Learning

Chess Metaphors for Business: Bruce Pandolfini

Starting position of chess game

Figure 7.1

Education is lifelong learning, and chess can be played one's whole life. The famous chess teacher Bruce Pandolfini regularly consults with executives in *Fortune* 500 companies. His book *Every Move Must Have a Purpose* (2003) highlights 15 chess principles that Pandolfini applies to business situations. For example, during a chess game, the psychological and physical clues one perceives can be misleading. The way one's opponent nervously rocks back and forth might be a sign of his distress over the game's progress. Or it might just be a bad habit. Pandolfini cautions his readers to rely on their judgment of the chess position, that is, "play the board, not the player" (p. 5). Similarly, in the business world, important decisions must have solid grounding in facts. Even in complicated chess positions or unclear markets, instincts honed through years of experience might be a guide through uncertainty. The patterns internalized (sometimes subconsciously) may be bringing the right answer to attention—as long as focus is kept on the chess board or the actual business dilemma.

Making plans is critical to chess and business, but small, flexible plans are more useful than diehard allegiance to a large, long-term plan. The best plans are composed of moves that "foil our opponent's aims while fostering ours" (p. 27). Clearly, Pandolfini's book is geared toward participants in competitive chess games and market economies. As he wrote, "Business, like chess, is a competition" (p. 50). Some of Pandolfini's advice applies to both competitive and noncompetitive chess scenarios. Pandolfini (2003) stated, "Operate on the assumption that you don't (or can't) make mistakes and you learn nothing at all" (p. 73). Only when you have connected actions with consequences, in chess and in life, will you grow wiser (rather than just growing older).

Senior Chess Players

Neil Charness found that older players (ages 50 to 65) have "decreases in efficiency in encoding and retrieval of information." Yet they can match the performance of younger players of similar ratings (Figure 7.2) by more efficient searches for solutions to chess problems (Charness, 1981, p. 37). The former director of the National Institute of Mental Health's Center on Aging, Gene Cohen, and other researchers on aging believe that

Carving out time to play games regularly may be every bit as valuable as forging the next deal or building a strong body. There's now good reason to think that people who engage in a lifetime of mental gymnastics build denser webs of neural connections than those who let their intellects coast. . . . People who challenge their minds, many researchers now believe, build a reserve capacity of brainpower they can draw on, like a retirement account, as they age. (Franklin, D., 1997, pp. 67–69)

Figure 7.2
Intergenerational match.
Copyright 2005 Bob Lindholm.

Smothered Mate Chess Game

On December 10, 1989, I played a game with a long combination that led to a **smothered mate**, a situation where the mated king cannot make legal moves because his own pieces occupy his possible escape squares. Of all my competitive chess games, this one most clearly shows planning on my part. I anticipated a smothered mate and made the moves necessary to get there. If you are a beginning chess player, read through Chapter 8 or an introductory chess book before playing through this chess game.

White: Alexey Root (USCF rating 2194). The mean of USCF ratings is 1500.
Black: Julie Wilson (USCF rating 1828).

Round Two, Southern California Chess Federation Women's Chess League. The Women's League was organized by Alina Markowski. It ran for three years. Women played on four different assigned four-player teams. One purpose of the league was to encourage the women to socialize. For example, we all went to lunch together on league play days.

Time Control: Game in 60 minutes, which means each player has 60 minutes to complete all of her moves.

Position after 14....e5?!

Figure 7.3

Position after 23....Nxe6

Figure 7.4

1. d4 Nf6
2. Nf3 e6
3. e3 b6
4. c4 Bb7
5. Nc3 d6 (Passive. Better to fight for the center with 5 . . . d5.)
6. Be2 Nbd7
7. 0-0 Be7
8. Nd2 0-0
9. f4 c5
10. Bf3 cxd4
11. exd4 Qc7
12. Bxb7 Qxb7
13. Qe2 d5
14. f5 e5?! (loses a pawn and opens up black for attack) (Figure 7.3)
15. dxe5 Bc5+
16. Kh1 Rfe8
17. Nf3 dxc4
18. e6! (shattering the pawns around black's king) (Figure 7.4) . . . fxe6
19. Qxc4 Kh8
20. fxe6 Nf8
21. Ng5 Qe7
22. Nd5 Nxd5

Position after 23....Nxe6

Figure 7.5

Position after 27....Qxe1

Figure 7.6

23. Qxd5 Nxe6 (Figure 7.5). Now the challenge for white is to bring her remaining pieces into the game. The most under-used pieces are usually the queen's bishop and the queen's rook, as is the case for white here.

24. Nf7+ Kg8

25. Bg5 Nxg5 (If Qc7, then Rae1 and Nd8.)

26. Nxg5+ (discovered check) Kh8

27. Rae1 Qxe1 (Figure 7.6)

28. Nf7+ Kg8

29. Nh6+ (double check) Kh8

30. Qg8+ Black resigned since smothered mate occurs after Rxg8.

31. Nf7 # or ++ (checkmate), 1-0. I anticipated the smothered mate combination on move 21. Chess players study mating positions so that they can aim for such wins. Knowledge helps one to plan effectively.

Chapter 8

LESSON PLANS

Third-Grade Beginner Plans

Two different approaches for teaching third graders chess are featured in the first half of this chapter. The first set (with three plans) includes the topics of algebraic notation and how the knight moves; how kings and rooks move and the two-rook checkmate; and how the queen moves and the differences between checkmate and **stalemate**. The second set (with four plans) includes the topics of etiquette for teaching chess and how the pawns move; the chess moves and the point values of pieces; and reading notated games. If you are not a chess player, studying these first seven lesson plans will give you a basic understanding of chess rules and concepts. Appendix B contains four worksheets that can be used with these first seven lesson plans. The worksheets are titled "Algebraic Notation," "Knight Moves," "King Moves," and "Two-Rook Mate." As discussed in more detail in Resources and References, there are other resources for chess problems and puzzles to share with your class. You might make your own chess worksheets with Chess Captor software at http://www.chesscaptor.com. You could purchase a book of chess worksheets or the Think Like a King® School Chess Software System, which allows students to practice chess moves on a computer. The worksheets I've created for Appendix B are not a complete introduction to chess rules, but they might function as a supplement to instruction or as homework.

The second half of Chapter 8, titled "Sample Plans for Other Grades," features lesson plans written by online students in Chess in the Classroom. Their plans have been modified for inclusion in this chapter and are arranged from easiest (in terms of chess knowledge required) to hardest. At the end of the chapter, I include two of my chess camp plans.

The Knight's Tour

■ *Objectives; organizing element: problem-solving*

Students use math to answer questions about the chessboard. Students learn algebraic notation, a coordinate geometry system of labeling chessboard squares. Students learn how a knight moves and try to solve a **knight's tour**. Students practice the TEKS mathematics problem-solving objective: understanding the problem, making a plan, carrying out the plan, evaluating the solution for reasonableness. (See Appendix A for equivalent problem-solving objectives for other states.)

The students to whom this lesson has been taught have had the background to solve problems dealing with coordinate geometry and with multiplication. By the middle of the third grade year, when this lesson was taught, students had completed a math unit on geometry that included locating points on a grid, three-dimensional shapes, and line segments. Most of the third graders had completed testing on the multiplication tables through 9×12.

A typical word problem on recent homework was to write a number sentence such as "Tim planted five rows of corn. There are six corn plants in each row. How many corn plants are there in all?" Correct answer: "$5 \times 6 = 30$ plants."

■ *Materials*

Demonstration board, blank chess diagrams, scratch paper, pencils.

■ *Procedure*

Students write down their answers to each of the following questions.

Question #1: How many squares are on a chessboard? Besides writing down your answer, write down how you figured it out. Some students may use counting; others may transfer their knowledge of multiplication to set up the equation $8 \times 8 = 64$.

Question #2: How many black (green) squares are on chessboard? Besides writing down your answer, write down how you figured it out.

Question #3: How would you describe this square (point to a square on the demonstration board, e.g., e4), so that someone not looking at the demonstration board could find it?

After students have shared their answers for questions #1 – #3 with the class, teach the algebraic notation system. In algebraic notation, one says the letter of the file first and then the number of the rank. Call on students to use notation to name squares.

■ *Blindfold square game*

The teacher calls a student up to the demonstration board. The teacher turns his or her back to the demonstration board. The student points to a square and says its algebraic name out loud. Without turning to look at the demonstration board, the teacher says out loud what color the named square is. For example, the square e4 (file e, rank 4) is a white square. The square g7 (file g, rank 7) is a black square. After the teacher demonstrates the activity, a student volunteer could try it. Have the student turn his back to the demonstration board, while another student points to a square on the demonstration board and names it for the volunteer. The volunteer then guesses or figures out what color the named square is. Then another volunteer has a turn to try.

■ *Notation lesson for the future*

The blindfold square game sets up future lessons on chess notation. As the students learn more about chess, they may want to read published chess games. When one writes down a chess move, one gives the name of the piece (Q = queen, R = rook, B = bishop, N = knight, K = king; a pawn isn't designated by a letter) and the square to which it moves. A pawn move to e4 is written e4; a knight move to e4 is written Ne4.

■ *The knight's moves*

Teach how the knight (N) moves. The N moves in the shape of a capital L. Have students signal thumbs up when N moves legally, thumbs down when not. The white X's in Figure 8.1 represent some of the N's choices. The N can move to c6, e6, f5, f3, c2, b3, or b5, or capture the black queen on e2, from the d4 square. The N can hop over its own or enemy pawns and pieces, and it captures the same way that it moves.

Start on the knight's tour worksheet, which is a blank chess diagram (Figure 8.2). Each student will then work individually on the knight's tour, writing the numeral one (1) where he or she starts the N, two (2) where it moves next, three (3) where it moves next, and so on, up to the possible 64 of a solved knight's tour. Any starting point for the N is possible for successful tour solution. It is typical for a student to get "stuck" on a knight's tour at about move 35. At that point, provide a fresh blank diagram for the student to try a different solution. When you photocopy the diagram, you may want to enlarge it for younger students. For older students, you could cut and paste several diagrams on one page, and then photocopy.

Legal moves of Knight (N) are X's

Or the N can take the queen on e2

Figure 8.1

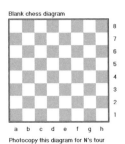

Blank chess diagram

Photocopy this diagram for N's tour

Figure 8.2

Checkmating with Two Rooks

The two-rook checkmate is a traditional choice for early chess instruction. Rook moves constrain the defending king's legal moves. Checkmate is delivered on a file or rank at the edge of the board. Each move by the defending king gives students immediate feedback as to the success or failure of their checkmating plan.

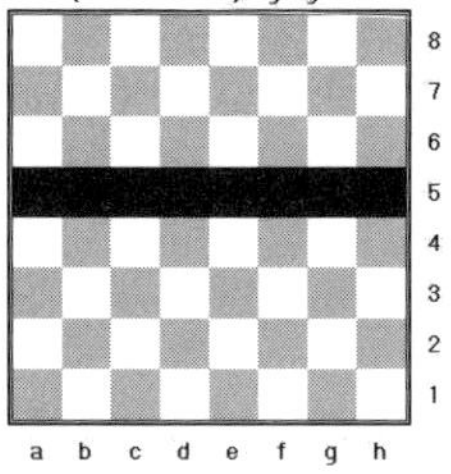

■ *Objectives; organizing element: flow*

Students learn and apply the terms vertical and horizontal as they learn how the rook moves. Students complete a two-rook checkmate. Practicing this mate could lead to flow for the students. Csikszentmihalyi (1990, p. 54) wrote, "The chess player's goals are equally obvious: to mate the opponent's king before his own is mated. With each move, he can calculate whether he has come closer to this objective."

■ *Materials*

Chess set and chessboard for every two students, blank paper, pens or pencils.

■ *Procedure*

Students write down the word *horizontal*, and draw a picture of a horizontal line. Students can also write a definition of the word *horizontal*. One way to remember the definition of horizontal is to think about the horizon of the earth, a flat line. On the chessboard, horizontal rows of squares are called ranks (see Figure 8.3).

Students write down the word *vertical* and draw a picture of a vertical line in relation to their horizontal line. Definition of vertical: "at right angles to the horizon." On the chessboard vertical sets of squares are called files (see Figure 8.4).

Figures 8.5 through 8.9 will enable you to demonstrate (a) how a rook moves: horizontally and vertically, back and forth, on ranks and files; (b) how a king moves, one square in any direction; and (c) how to use two rooks to checkmate the king. In Figure 8.5, the legal moves of the black king are represented by black X's. In Figure 8.6, the white rook on a5 controls the entire a-file and the entire 5th rank. The rook can move to (and also controls) all the squares with white X's. The black king cannot move to the squares with white X's because he cannot move into check. However, he can still move to the squares with the black X's.

In Figure 8.7, the additional pieces required for the two-rook checkmate have been added to the chessboard. The white king is not actually required to complete this mate, but having both kings on the chessboard makes the position legal. In Figure 8.7, the white rook on h6 can move to the squares with white X's that are on the h-file and on the 6th rank. The white rook on a5, as in Figure 8.6., can move to the squares on the a-file and 5th rank that have white X's. The white rook on h6 is checking the black king. The black king cannot move to d6

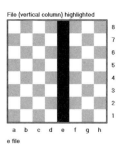

Rank (horizontal row) highlighted

5th rank

Figure 8.3

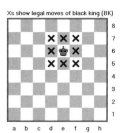

File (vertical column) highlighted

e file

Figure 8.4

Xs show legal moves of black king (BK)

Figure 8.5

BK can move to d6, f6, f7, e7, or d7

White X's show legal moves of WR

Figure 8.6

Figure 8.7

Figure 8.8

Figure 8.9

Figure 8.10

(the circle in Figure 8.7) because of the white rook on h6. The king must move to the squares with black X's, as those squares are not controlled by the enemy rooks. The move shown on the board is "1. Rh6+," which reads "Move one: rook to h6; check."

In Figure 8.8, the black king has moved out of the check from the h6 rook, 1. . . . Ke7. But now white's second move is 2. Ra7+. The black king will retreat to d8, e8, or f8 (labeled with black X's) because he cannot move to any square attacked (controlled) by an enemy rook. The squares that the white rooks control are not marked in Figure 8.8 to simplify the look of the diagram.

In Figure 8.9, the black king has moved to e8 (2. . . . Ke8) and white has responded with 3. Rh8++. The king is in checkmate (denoted by ++ or #) because he cannot escape from the check given by the R on h8. The h8 rook controls all the 8th-rank squares, and the a7 rook controls all the 7th-rank squares.

■ *Practice*

Students in pairs practice the two-rook checkmate. First one student has the two rooks; then (after checkmate) the other student gets the two rooks. The starting position can be varied as to level of difficulty depending on the students' understanding. A difficult starting position is shown in Figure 8.10. The black king's central placement means the white rooks have to work together for several moves to drive him to the edge of the board. An easier starting position would be either Figure 8.7 or Figure 8.8, where the black king is only a couple of moves away from being checkmated.

Checkmate and Stalemate

■ *Objectives; organizing element: multiple intelligences*

This lesson has students comparing and contrasting the use of a checklist of characteristics. In chess, checkmate and stalemate are key concepts. Being able to compare and contrast checkmate and stalemate is a skill similar to differentiating between a complete sentence and a sentence fragment. Students must look at many examples before becoming efficient at differentiating checkmate from stalemate, complete sentence from fragment. Students review vertical and horizontal when reviewing the two-rook checkmate. At the end of the lesson, students work individually (on the knight's tour) or with a partner (reviewing the two-rook checkmate).

Gardner advocated using multiple intelligences to learn academic concepts. In this cooperative group lesson plan, students use their interpersonal intelligence to find answers to chess problems. Using spatial and linguistic intelligences, students translate the algebraically notated chess positions on the chalkboard into correct piece placement on their boards. The skill is similar to having written directions to a location, and then tracing those streets on a map or driving the route. Logical mathematical intelligence helps students determine if each position meets the given criteria for checkmate, stalemate, or neither. Students manipulate the pawns and pieces on the chessboard, exercising bodily kinesthetic intelligence in their search for the meaning of each chess position.

■ *Materials*

Supply each chessboard with one black king, one black rook, one black knight, one white king, one white queen, and two white rooks.

■ *Procedure*

Warm up by reviewing the two-rook checkmate on the demonstration board with the whole class. Have students call out rook moves to mate the lone king on the demonstration board in the two-rook mate. Each student volunteering a rook move will tell whether their suggested rook move is vertical or horizontal.

Students will differentiate between *stalemate* (a deadlock; stale = lacking in freshness, impaired in strength; definition in chess is "one side has no legal moves but is not in check") and *checkmate* ("king is in check and cannot escape/no legal moves"). Stalemate counts as a draw or half a point. Checkmate counts as a win, worth a full point.

The written chalkboard instructions tell students how to set up the chessboards on each of the four classroom tables. Figures 8.11 through 8.14 represent the chessboard positions on the four tables. In each figure, it is black's turn to move.

The position is checkmate

White has just played Qg7 ++

Figure 8.11

This position is check, but not checkmate

White has just played Rg7+

Figure 8.12

Black can move his N; not stalemate

Black to move

Figure 8.13

White has just played Rh8++

White mated using the two rook mate

Figure 8.14

- The written instructions for students to set up Figure 8.11 are "Table 1: white Kh6, Qg7; black Ra4, Nd4, Kg8."
- The written instructions for students to set up Figure 8.12 are "Table 2: white Rg7, Kg6; black Kg8."
- The written instructions for students to set up Figure 8.13 are "Table 3: white Rc7, Re7, Kd4; black Nh5, Kd8."
- The written instructions for students to set up Figure 8.14 are "Table 4: white Ke6, Rg7, Rh8; black Ke8, Ne1."

The differences between stalemate and checkmate will be discussed and listed on the chalkboard. Stalemate means that the defending king is not in check, and yet there are no legal moves for the defender. Stalemate is a draw or tie. Checkmate means the defending king is under attack (check) by an enemy piece. In checkmate, the defending king cannot escape (move away from) the check, capture the checking piece, or block the check.

After the whole class discussion, to understand the difference between these two concepts, teams of students will study four positions. One position will be on each table (or set of desks large enough to accommodate a chessboard). Each team will figure out the characteristics of the table position in front of them. Roles for each team member:

Legal moves of the white queen are X's

Or the WQ can capture Ng1

Figure 8.15

one person in charge of making sure the position on the table is as stated in algebraic notation in the chalkboard directions; one person in charge of seeing if the defending king is in check; one person in charge of seeing whether there are legal moves for the defender; one person at each table writing down whether the position is checkmate, stalemate or neither; and one person in charge of making sure the pawns and pieces are set up in the correct position for the next team. Then, after 5 minutes each team moves to the next chess position.

■ *Closure*

After each team has rotated to each table's chess position, discuss their results as a whole class. Figure 8.11 (Table 1) is a checkmate because the queen can move and attack multiple squares in any direction (see Figure 8.15). In the Figure 8.11, the white queen is attacking the enemy (black) king and the king cannot escape from her attack. Every move he might make falls under her control, and he can't move into check. For the same reason, the black king cannot capture the white queen. Because she is defended by the white king, such a capture by the black king would violate the rule about not moving into check. Finally, it is not possible to block the white queen's check because there is no empty square between the white queen and the black king. Figure 8.12 (Table 2) is a check, but not a checkmate. The black king is attacked by the white rook, but can move out of check by either . . . Kf8 or . . . Kh8. So the answer for Table 2 is "neither checkmate nor stalemate." Figure 8.13 (Table 3) is not stalemate. The black king cannot move, since the white rooks cover all his possible moves, but black can still move his knight. So the answer for Table 3 is "neither." Figure 8.14 (Table 4) is a two-rook checkmate, as taught previously.

Discuss other draws (e.g., king against king), or draws that are agreed upon because the players want to stop playing in a fairly equal game. During the remaining time, students choose whether they want to review the two-rook checkmate with a partner or work on the knight's tour individually on blank chess diagrams.

Chess Etiquette and the Square of the Pawn

■ *Objectives; organizing elements: interpersonal intelligence and visualization*

Students learn the first part of chess etiquette: how to behave during teaching or analysis sessions. (A second part of chess etiquette—how to behave during a competitive chess game—should be introduced before students begin tournaments or an after-school club.) Students learn how a king moves and how a pawn moves. Students learn that a pawn promotes to another piece—a Q = queen, R = rook, N = knight, or B = bishop—upon reaching the 8th rank.

Correct orientation of the chessboard, with the white pieces along the first rank and the square in the bottom right corner being a white color, is discussed. Students solve a problem using their mind's eye. That is, they visualize whether a king can capture a pawn in particular situations. Two methods of visualization—counting and the "square of the pawn"—are discussed at the end of the lesson. Interpersonal intelligence is used when exercising etiquette for teaching situations. Visualization is important for solving the king-and-pawn exercise.

■ *Materials*

Algebraically labeled chessboards and chess sets (one for every two students) and a demonstration board.

■ *Procedure*

Chess etiquette encompasses behavior during analysis (postmortem or other learning) situations and behavior during a competitive chess game. Have the students define what makes someone a polite chess tutor. Write answers on the dry erase or chalk board. Answers might include welcoming the student by shaking hands, learning the student's name, and making encouraging remarks after the interaction. Make analogies to the classroom and to sports activities (e.g., PE learning environment vs. a competitive basketball game).

Teach how a king moves and how a pawn moves. A pawn may move one or two squares on its first move, and one square on each move thereafter. Although it moves to the front, it captures diagonally. Thus in Figure 8.16, with white to move, the white pawn could capture the black bishop on d3 or the black knight on f3. Or the white pawn could instead choose to move to e3 or to e4.

When a white pawn reaches the 8th rank, it is promoted to a Q, R, N, or B. The same thing happens when a black pawn reaches the 1st rank, as black pawns travel from the 7th rank to the first rank to promote. There is a special move for pawns, en passant, that won't be discussed in this lesson.

Present a problem with just a black chess king and a white chess pawn. White will move the pawn to h5 (see the white X in Figure 8.17). The problem to be solved is, "Can black capture white in the future?" Black's best move is king to e5 (the black X in Figure 8.17). What will white do next? And then what will black do? After students solve this first problem, discovering that the black king will capture the white pawn just as it promotes, give another similar problem or two.

Split the class in half. Half of the class will be "problem creators." That is, they will create a chess position on their chessboard in which the only components are a black king and a white pawn, and it will be white's move. The other half of the class will be "problem solvers." They will travel around to each problem creator. When a solver arrives at a creator's problem, the creator asks the solver what he or she thinks

Legal moves of the WP are X's

WP can also capture either Bd3 or Nf3

Figure 8.16

WP will move to h5

White to move

Figure 8.17

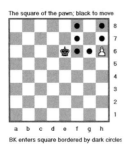

The square of the pawn; black to move

BK enters square bordered by dark circles

Figure 8.18

the solution is. Then the two play out the position, with the solver taking the role of the white pawn and moving first. Monitor the activity, looking for politeness and accurate problem formulation in the problem creators. See if the problem solvers are getting the answers right.

■ *The square of the pawn*

As a class we will discuss how the students solved the problem. Most will probably say they counted in their heads; that is, "If white moves here, black moves here. Then white moves here, black moves here." Show a new way to visualize a solution, the "square of the pawn." If the black king cannot get inside the square of the pawn, the king will not be able to catch up with and capture the pawn. It is black to move in Figure 8.18. In this case, with black to move, the black king can get inside the square and will capture the pawn. Comment on the politeness of the problem creators and the efficacy of the problem solvers.

Legal Moves and Point Values of Pieces

■ *Objectives; organizing elements: interpersonal intelligence and visualization*

Students learn to recognize all the pieces and pawns, are exposed to their point values, and get an introduction to how each piece or pawn moves and captures. Interpersonal intelligence is exercised during the creator/solver exercise. Visualization is needed for the blindfold square game and for the square of the pawn.

■ *Materials*

Demonstration board, chessboards, pawns, and pieces.

■ *Procedure*

As the students arrive in class, play the blindfold square game. Ask students how they solved the K vs. P exercise from last lesson. Then review the square of the pawn concept. Then the students will finish the creator/solver exercise from last time, taking the role that they didn't have previously.

After the students complete the creator/solver exercise, reconvene the whole class in front of the demonstration board. Ask students questions about each chess piece. The questions will cover how many points (pawns) the piece/pawn is worth, the name of the piece, the abbreviation for the piece, how the piece moves, and how the piece captures. Special moves of the king and the pawn will be mentioned. This question-and-answer session with students will serve as a lecture for the whole class. Create Figure 8.19 on the dry erase board as students give answers to your questions.

Figure 8.19

Chart of piece names, values, and powers.

Name/ Points	King (K)/ infinite	Queen (Q)/9	Rook (R)/5	Bishop (B)/3.25	Knight (N)/3	Pawn (P)/1
Moves	One square any direction	Horizontal, vertical, diagonal	Horizontal, vertical	Diagonal	L-shaped	One or two squares forward on first move; one square forward thereafter.
Special powers or restrictions	Castling; may not move into check, or castle over check		Castling		Hops over pieces and pawns	Promotes on 8th rank (to Q, R, B, or N); captures on diagonal only; en passant.

Chess "Trading Card" Game

■ *Objectives; organizing elements: creativity and interpersonal intelligence*

Students will collaborate to teach each other about one particular piece or pawn. Students will read the chart and, if necessary, refer to a chess book to figure out how their piece moves. Students will make a product (cards) to represent that piece or pawn. Students will then trade cards with each other. To complete a trade, students must show each other on a chessboard how a particular piece or pawn moves, captures, and what (if any) special powers it has. Students will teach each other how each piece or pawn moves, captures, its point value, and any special powers it has. Creativity is needed to come up with ideas for cards, and interpersonal intelligence is used in the cooperative group work.

■ *Materials*

Index cards, scratch paper, laminated poster of Figure 8.19 ("Chart of piece names, values, and powers"), sample trading card, pencils, chess sets and boards, demonstration board, and classroom set of chess books for beginners.

■ *Procedure*

Self-described knowledgeable students are assigned to the table of a chess piece or pawn. The tables are labeled king, queen, rook, bishop, knight, and pawn. After the knowledgeable students are assigned to tables, the other students are sorted equally among those tables. Each table thus ends up with one knowledgeable student plus several others.

Before the students move to the tables, they are told that at each table they have to create and manufacture cards about their assigned piece or pawn. The card should tell: how many points (pawns) the piece/

pawn is worth, the name of the piece, abbreviation for the piece, how the piece moves, and how the piece captures.

Any special powers of the piece (such as en passant or castling) should also be noted on the card. Each table is in charge of designing and producing one sample card, and then ultimately enough cards to share with each of their classmates. Before they are allowed to start producing cards, the knowledgeable student must review the moves and properties of the table's assigned piece or pawn with his or her group members. The students can consult the laminated poster of "chart of piece names, values, and powers." Pamphlets or books with chess rules, if available, can be distributed to each table as extra resources. Students should also practice the moves on chessboards. The tables with special powers (pawn, king, rook) need to practice those special moves (en passant, castling) to be ready.

Each group makes a sample card highlighting its assigned piece or pawn. When everyone in the group feels they are ready to be tested and that their sample card is good, the teacher tests their knowledge and views their card. Then the group is authorized to start producing cards. Inform group members that they must divide the following four jobs among the group members: (1) cut out and glue or tape the diagrams to the front of the index cards; (2) draw the diagrammed pawns and pieces (circle black pawns and pieces); (3) write on the back of the card the rules for piece moves and captures, and any special powers the piece has; (4) set up the chessboard for visitors to the table and prepare a lesson for teaching the visitors about the piece. This fourth role could also be preparing slogans, art, or enticements for the visitor to feel welcome to the table.

Blank chess diagrams will be ready to be cut and taped onto the front (unlined) side of the index cards. When producing a card, the students will show on the diagram how their assigned piece moves and how it captures. The students can either draw a picture of the piece or use its abbreviation. The standard way to make diagrams is to circle the names of the black pieces and pawns (e.g., ® for a black rook). In contrast, the symbol for a white rook on a hand-written diagram is an R. Each group of students will have a sample card for their piece/pawn to use as a model. Figure 8.20 shows the front of a sample bishop trading card. On the lined back of the index card, write that the bishop is worth 3+ pawns, and that its name is abbreviated B. The bishop doesn't have any special powers.

The trading card game begins after each table has produced enough cards to give one to each member of the class. It is described within the next lesson plan.

Reading Chess

■ *Objectives; TEKS*

Students will learn how to read short, algebraically notated chess games. Students will take notes on the games. Students will define

Legal moves of the Bishop (B) are Xs

Or the B can capture Black P on h7

Figure 8.20

White to move and mate in one

1. Rh4#

Figure 8.21

checkmate. Students will conclude the trading card game exercise, and through that exercise learn from others how each piece moves. TEKS (see Appendix A for equivalent standards from other states): (a) Reading/ text structures/literary concepts: The student analyzes the characteristics of various types of texts (genres). The student is expected to identify the purposes of different types of texts, such as to inform, influence, express, or entertain; (b) Problem solving (mathematics): Understanding the problem, making a plan, carrying out the plan, evaluating the solution for reasonableness.

■ *Materials*

Trading cards, chess sets, demonstration board, pencils, and paper.

■ *Procedure*

What are the purposes of reading? As students list the purposes of reading, steer their answers toward state standards regarding the purposes of texts. Students consider silently the warm-up problem in Figure 8.21, posted on the demonstration board. Note: Post the chess pieces in position, but don't give out the 1. Rh4++ answer.

Comment that checkmate is the object of the game of chess. It occurs when the defending king is in check (under attack) and can't escape the check by blocking the check, by moving out of check, or by capturing the checking piece. Call on a student to give the solution to the warm-up problem, 1. Rh4# (In words, "Rook to h4; checkmate.") Tell the class, "Today we will learn to read something new: chess games. You will be writing down these games so that you can review the information and later share it with other students. Keep the definition of checkmate in mind, and raise your hand if you can tell me white's plan after move three." Here is the first game: **Scholar's mate**. Write the moves on the dry erase board, and call on students to come up and make the written move on the demonstration board.

1. e4 e5. If students aren't too confident about the legal moves of pawns and pieces, use long notation: 1. e2-e4 e7-e5, and so on. Long notation, listing both the "to" and "from" squares of a move, ensures that legal moves are made: in other words, that it is a pawn on e2 (not one on f2) that gets moved to e4.

2. Bc4 Bc5, 3. Qh5 Nf6, 4. Qxf7#. The "x" in notation indicates that the move is a capture. The "x" is optional; the move could be written Qf7#. Discuss how white threatened checkmate and then executed it. Ask students to write down the game.

Use the language of problem solving to discuss this second game, Legal's mate. Legal's mate is a mating sequence that appeared in the game between M. de Kermar Legall and Saint Brie in about 1750: **1. e4 e5, 2. Bc4 d6, 3. Nf3 Bg4, 4.Nc3 g6, 5.Nxe5 Bxd1, 6.Bxf7+ Ke7, 7. Nd5#.** As with the first game, the teacher writes the moves on the dry erase board. Students come up to the demonstration board to make the moves. Finally, students copy down the moves in their notes.

After these two games have been shown, recommence the trading card activity. One person from each table ventures to the other tables to earn the cards. The remaining members of the trading card company teach and test visitors about their table's piece or pawn. When a visitor comes to the table, the table members show how their piece or pawn moves, share poetry or slogans or art about their piece, and then test the visitor about the piece. If the visitor learns the information, he or she is given a trading card. When a visitor has collected all the trading cards from the other tables, he or she returns to his or her home table. Then another person from the home table is allowed to visit the other tables.

At the end of the lesson, everyone should have six cards (K, Q, R, B, N, and P). The cards can be used between chess lesson times to review how each piece or pawn moves. Today's short chess games can be reviewed to practice notation and checkmate.

Sample Plans for Other Grades

Graph of Piece Values

Plan by Bryan Sears, the University of Texas at Dallas (2005).

■ *Objectives*

The objectives are to (a) recognize the pawns and pieces, and (b) learn their values.

■ *Student population: elementary school beginning chess players*

■ *Materials*

Chess set for each student; paper, markers or crayons.

■ *Procedure*

Show the students each chessman, name it, and ask them to repeat its name. Allow the students to feel the pawns and pieces so they can recognize them by touch as well. Show the pieces' value in terms of points with pawn = 1, knight = 3, bishop = 3.25, rook = 5, queen = 9, and king = infinity. Inform them that points stand for pawns; a pawn is worth one pawn, a knight is worth three pawns, and so on. Give them graph paper and ask them to color in the value (0–9) for all the pieces in a chart fashion. Figure 8.22 could serve as a model for their chart.

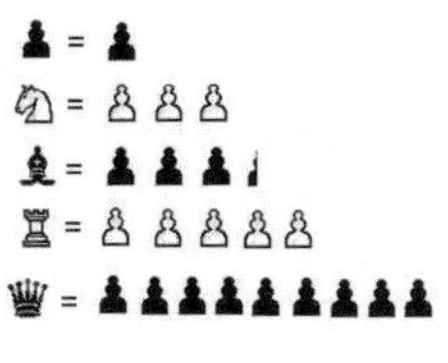

Then go over the values once again verbally. Next, mix pawns and pieces together and ask students to give the values by adding. Tell them that for the adding exercise the bishop's value will be rounded off to 3 points. For instance, select a pawn, a bishop, and a rook and let them add those values to 9. Ask the students to find any combinations of chess

Figure 8.22

figures that add up to a certain number. For example, the number 7 would require what pawns and pieces?

Chessboard Bingo

Plan by Linda Noble, the University of Texas at Dallas (2005).

■ *Objectives; TEKS*

Students learn to position a chessboard, the ranks of the chessboard, and the files of the chessboard. By finding a point on the board, the students practice the following TEKS: 3.15 (A) identify the mathematics in everyday situations; 3.10 recognize that numbers can be represented by points on a line.

■ *Student population: upper elementary school beginning chess players*

■ *Materials*

Chessboards (one for each student), demonstration board for teacher, 64 paper chessboards, bingo chessboards, bingo markers. Teacher resource: *Chess for Dummies* (2005) by James Eade, pp. 14–17.

■ *Procedure*

First let the students examine the chessboard and then share with them the proper way to position the chessboard, putting the white square in the right-hand corner. Explain to the students the difference between files and ranks. Explain that the files and ranks give a unique identifier to every square using what is called the file first method.

To practice together, the students position their chessboards with the white square in the right-hand corner. The teacher also orients her demonstration board correctly. The students and the teacher pick certain squares and identify them using the file first method, making sure the students understand why each square is identified that way. The students and the teacher will also identify different diagonals, such as h1 to a8, on their chessboards.

For independent practice, the students will spin their chessboards and then position them in the proper position to play chess. The teacher can walk around the room to monitor the chessboards' positioning. The students will then label squares on paper versions of 64 chessboards. The students can label up to 64 paper chessboards, writing one square label on each board (i.e., labeling "e4" on one paper board, "g2" on the next board, etc.). There will be some duplicate squares on the paper chessboards gathered up at the end of 5 minutes of labeling. They are deposited in a hat or a box for the next activity.

As a fun way to conclude the lesson, and to reinforce locating squares algebraically on chessboards, the students and the teacher play bingo. Students receive a bingo chessboard. Just like in a regular bingo game, certain squares are blacked out on each student's bingo chessboard. If bingo chess is going to be played more than one time, the teacher might want to laminate the bingo chessboards. In addition to one bingo chessboard, each student gets a supply of plastic bingo markers (checkers would work) for marking off squares on his or her bingo chessboard. As the teacher draws out of the hat or box, she calls the squares out loud. The students mark the squares that they have available on their particular bingo chessboards. The object of chessboard bingo will be to get 5 squares or points in a row vertically, horizontally, or diagonally. The student who achieves this calls out "Bingo." After students clear off the bingo markers and the paper chessboards are put back in the hat or box, bingo can begin again.

Classifying the Kingdom

Plan by Josh Eaton (2005).

■ *Objectives; Florida state standards*

Students will use science to understand the classification of chess pawns and pieces. Florida Sunshine State Standards (Science Grades 3–8): SC.G.1.3. Students will understand that the classification of living things is based on a given set of criteria and is a tool for understanding biodiversity and interrelationships. SC.F.1.2. Students will know that living things are different but share similar structures.

■ *Student population middle school science, special education, some chess knowledge*

This lesson plan debuted with a grade 6, ESE (special education), self-contained science class at Gulf Middle school in Port Richey, FL. Prior chess experience: Students were beginners at the game of chess. They had previously been taught only the names and functions of the chess pawns and pieces. This plan could be adapted to other elementary or middle school science classes.

■ *Materials*

"Classifying Animals" spreadsheet, student computers, plastic baggies, chess pawns and pieces. Construct the "Classifying Animals" spreadsheet by listing the categories of fish, amphibians, bird, reptiles, and mammals across the top. Along the side list the following descriptions: warm-blooded or cold-blooded; type of body covering; live birth or hatched from an egg; feed young with milk (yes/no); has a skeleton or no skeleton; breathe with lungs or with gills.

■ *Science procedure*

As the students enter the room, their daily "do now" question already written on the board is "Classify the following things into groups containing similar characteristics: person, penguin, shark, dog, ostrich, snake, frog, dolphin, salamander, turtle." The students have 5 minutes to complete the do now question.

The teacher begins a whole class discussion by defining what classification is: The arrangement of objects, ideas, or information into groups, the members of which have one or more characteristics in common. Point out why classifying living things is important: Classification makes things easier to find, identify, and study. Introduce the five main classifications for animals (fish, amphibians, reptiles, birds, and mammals).

After 15 minutes of discussion, the students begin a three-step animal classification activity. This activity uses computers for steps two and three.

Step 1: Distribute a copy of the spreadsheet entitled "Classifying Animals" to each student.
Step 2: Students are to use the following Web sites to research the given characteristics of each of the five main animal classes: http://www.factmonster.com; http://falcon.jmu.edu/~ramseyil/vertebrates.htm; http://www.fi.edu/tfi/units/life/classify/classify.html.
Step 3: Throughout their research, students should fill in the "Classifying Animals" spreadsheet with the information they locate on each animal class. The three steps should be completed in about 15 minutes.

Once the animal classification activity is complete, instructor should lead a 5-minute discussion highlighting students' findings. Instructor should not only incorporate discussion about findings, but also encourage students to think of animals that would fall into each of the five classes. Or the instructor could say the name of an animal and ask students to use their "Classifying Animals" spreadsheet to classify the animal.

■ *Chess procedure*

Chess pawns and pieces can be classified in much the same manner as animals. They can be lumped into similar classes based on their movements allowed, the number of steps each move includes, or their physical characteristics. For this lesson, physical characteristics are used.

The chess piece classification activity should take about 15 minutes.

Step 1: Students are split into pairs and given plastic baggies.
Step 2: Students collaboratively group pieces and pawns together according to their physical characteristics. (For example, a white pawn and a black pawn are bagged together if the pair uses "shape" as the classifying physical characteristic.)
Step 3: Class discussion, where pairs of students explain their classification of the chess figures based on a physical criterion (shape or size).

Chess Charades

Plan by William Gray and Chasity Butler (2004).

■ *Objectives; bodily kinesthetic and interpersonal intelligences*

Students identify the characteristics of chessmen by playing a game of chess charades. Students use both bodily kinesthetic intelligence and interpersonal intelligence.

■ *Student population: upper elementary and middle school, some chess knowledge*

This 30-minute lesson is appropriate for upper elementary and middle school students who have already been taught the movements and names of the chess pieces and pawns.

■ *Materials*

Large area for acting out charades, dry erase or chalkboard for keeping track of score, stopwatch or watch with a timer.

■ *Procedure*

The instructor begins by introducing the procedure and object of the game of charades. The game of charades is played by having one member of the team starting off and acting out the role or characteristic of a chosen chessman (this piece or pawn will be chosen by the instructor). The actor is allowed to use gestures and movement, but not voice. His or her team must guess which piece or pawn his or her teammate is by using their knowledge of game piece functions or characteristics. If a team guesses the correct answer within 10 seconds, that team gets 2 points. If the guess is wrong, the other team has 2 seconds to steal by guessing correctly. A steal earns 1 point for the stealing team.

The instructor will divide the students into two groups with equal numbers of students on each team. One person from each team will be selected at a time to be an actor. Students will take turns in a rotation. The instructor will keep score on the dry erase or chalkboard and time the actors.

The instructor should see not only how well students act out pawns and pieces, but also how well students guess. The students' performances at charades provide one indication of how well students learned chess information in prior lessons.

Problem Solving in Math and in Chess

Plan by Alanna Arenivas, Elementary Math Coordinator, Dallas Independent School District (2001).

■ *Objectives*

(a) Compare problem-solving steps in math to moves in chess; (b) investigate development of pieces in traditional chess openings; (c) create openings that follow chess development principles.

■ *Student population: fifth graders who have some chess knowledge*

Fifth graders who have already learned piece names, piece value, piece moves, and algebraic notation are the intended audience for this lesson.

■ *Materials*

Chessboards, pawns, and pieces; demonstration board. Teacher's resource: *Chess for Dummies* (pp. 41–53, 155–165) by James Eade (2005).

■ *Procedure*

Write the equation $1 + y > 5$ on the chalkboard. Discuss the solution set to the equation. Guide the discussion to the generalization that there are an infinite number of members in the solution set. Draw an analogy to chess: Just as there are numerous possibilities for y that will complete the equation and make it true, there are numerous moves in chess that contribute to the successful completion of a game.

Next present the following story problem on transparency to the class: Alex bought a dozen avocados for $0.38 apiece and 2 pounds of tomatoes for $0.79 a pound at the fruit market. He gave the cashier a $20 bill. How much change should he receive?

Discuss the multiple steps that must be completed in order to answer the question. To solve the grocery store problem, one could begin by calculating the avocado cost first. Or one could start by figuring out the cost of the tomatoes. Nevertheless, one cannot start by subtracting from $20. That step has to wait until the avocado and tomato calculations are done.

Draw an analogy to chess. The beginning moves in chess don't have to be completed in a specific order. Yet certain moves have to be made before other moves are possible. For example, one has to move pawns before one can move bishops. In chess openings, one tries to control the center of the board. So typical first moves are 1.e4 or 1. d4, followed by N moves to f3 and c3. However, it's also possible to play 1. Nf3 followed by 2. d4, just as one could decide to calculate tomatoes before avocados. In chess, bishops are developed next. After the minor pieces (bishops and knights) are activated, kingside castling often occurs. But sometimes one castles before developing the queen's bishop. Solicit additional comparisons from the students.

Discuss "maximizing the power of the pieces in a minimum amount of time" (*Chess for Dummies*, p. 156). Focus on controlling the center of the board versus the wings. Demonstrate popular opening moves in contrast to poor opening moves.

Simulate the beginning of a game on the demonstration board. Call on students to classify different moves in terms of their effectiveness of controlling the center. Distribute chessboards. Pair students. Instruct the students to play and record their and their partner's first five moves. Explain each pair of students will present and defend their openings.

After the students have had enough time to play and record five moves, collect the chessboards and reconvene the whole class. Then allow at least one group to present their created opening to the class on the demonstration board.

Mobility

Plan by Barry Keith, Charlottesville, Virginia (2001).

■ *Objective*

Students will learn that the point value of chess pieces is a function of their **mobility**.

■ *Student population: upper elementary students and older with prior knowledge of how the chess pieces move*

■ *Materials*

A chess set and board, and pencil and paper for each pair of players. A demonstration board may be useful.

■ *Procedure*

Ask students if they know how many "points" of value are assigned to chess pieces. If this is a new idea, suggest that the pawn be 1 point, and solicit ideas for other values. Students may give a list similar to pawn = 1, knight = 3, bishop = 3, rook = 5, and queen = 9. Mention that some people think the bishop is closer to 3.25 points, and perhaps the queen is closer to 10. Mention that players consider the points a guide for the fair exchange of pieces.

Have students brainstorm ideas to questions like What should you capture if you give up your bishop? What if you give up your queen? How about your rook and your pawn?

Ask if students know how these point values have been determined. How do they know that one piece is worth more points than another? Perhaps one will say that a queen can move to a lot more different squares than a pawn, for example.

Define mobility of pieces as the ability to move from one square to others. Ask students which pieces have the most mobility. Illustrate the queen's mobility on an empty board. For example, if the queen is placed on an outside square (on the "a" or "h" files, or on the 1st or 8th ranks), she can go to 21 different squares. If she is placed in the area bounded by b2, g2, g7, and b7, she can move to 23 squares. On the square bounded by c3, f3, f6, and c6, she can move to 25 squares. In one of the four central squares, she can go to 27. So the queen's average mobility on an empty board is $[(21 \times 28) + (23 \times 20) + (25 \times 12) + (27 \times 4)]/64 = 22.75$. Illustrate the "rings" on the chessboard for visual learners, and write up the computation.

Pair up students and assign each pair a chessboard. The pairs are to make mobility calculations for the rook, bishop, knight, and pawn, ranking them from least mobile to most mobile. They should find the rook easy, as it has access to 14 squares from everywhere on the board. The bishop can move between 7 and 13 squares on an empty board, and the knight from 2 to 8. The pawn does not control the square in front of it, so it really attacks only two squares. An "a" or "h" pawn attacks just one square. Students should see similarities in the figures for mobility and those for the point values. For example, the rook's mobility is somewhat more than half that of the queen. The bishop's mobility is more than half that of the rook, and about a third of that for the queen.

Reconvene the whole class. Ask why the knight is considered the equal of the bishop, though his mobility is less. If this question stumps students, ask what color square each piece can control. Point out that the bishop can only control half the board's squares, whereas the knight changes square color on each move and can eventually reach all of them. While the bishop has more range, the knight has jumping ability. Explain that the bishop and the knight are equal in general, though one or the other might be better for certain kinds of positions. For example, a knight might be better when there are many pawn chains on the board, because the bishop's mobility is lessened by the locked pawn structure whereas the knight can maneuver over and around the pawn chains.

King and Pawn Dance

■ *Objective; organizing element: bodily kinesthetic intelligence*

Teach how to draw with a king and pawn versus king, with learning reinforced by a dance. Bodily kinesthetic intelligence, using one's whole body to fashion a product, is featured in this plan. The product is a dance expressing how to draw a particular chess endgame.

■ *Student population: elementary school students who know the rules of chess*

Many children who know the rules of chess, and even some who compete often in scholastic chess tournaments, don't know basic king and pawn endgames. This lesson plans teaches the typical K + P vs. K draw pattern. Coming in to the lesson, students need to have an understanding of how the kings and pawns move, and that a pawn promotes to a Q, R, B, or N upon reaching its 8th rank. They also need to know how to write chess notation.

■ *Materials*

Demonstration board, chess sets, boards, diagram sheets, score sheets, pencils, crowns, sidewalk chalk; sidewalk, basketball court, or asphalt parking lot.

■ *Procedure*

Have students copy down the position in Figure 8.23 on to a blank chess diagram. Have the students vote on whether this position is a draw.

Figure 8.23

Figure 8.24

Figure 8.25

Figure 8.26

Then have the students play out the position, keeping notation on their scoresheets. Discuss their results. Then demonstrate how the king and pawn versus king endgame is, in this case, a draw (whether it is white or black to move). The draw is achieved when black stalemates himself.

Have students take the king and pawn draw (which is like a dance) outside for practice. Students will draw a chessboard on the cement or asphalt using chalk. Paper crowns will designate the students acting out the king parts. Notice how, in the following diagrams, the black king often steps just opposite the white king. The feel is like a dance, because the black king must anticipate the white king's moves and respond correctly to them. In our example, black (the black king, or BK) moved first.

By moving straight back to e7, black plans to stop white's king from controlling the crucial squares in front of the white pawn. If white moves to f5, black will counter with a king move to f7. Then the white king would not be able to go forward to e6, f6, or g6. In Figure 8.25, white chooses to move his king to d5 and black steps opposite him to d7, thus controlling e6, d6, and c6. The control black takes is called the **opposition**. Because black has the opposition, white must retreat his king or push his pawn forward.

After 2. . . . Kd7, the white king (WK) is blocked from forward progress. That is, the black king (BK) prevents the WK from moving to e6, d6, and c6. Since the WK can't make progress toward supporting his pawn's journey, white moves with his pawn (WP) instead (Figure 8.26). Then the pattern first seen in Figure 8.23 reappears, just one square further down the board (Figure 8.27). The pattern of moves repeats (Figures 8.28 and 8.29). In Figure 8.30, white has two main choices of final move. The pictured diagram shows white stalemating with 7. Ke6. Stalemate is a draw. Alternative WK moves at move 7 lose the pawn to the BK (one of those is shown in Figure 8.31). Once the BK captures the WP, the position is a draw as no one can win K vs. K.

Battleship Chess

Recently I read about "Battleship Game" (Pelts & Alburt, 1992), which is a drill to help students memorize the algebraic notation of squares. My battleship chess drill has a completely different focus and different rules for play.

■ *Objective; organizing element: problem solving*

Students experiment with different king and pawn formations, and deduce which formation is best.

■ *Student population: chess club members, all ages*

The West Covina (southern California) chess club in the late 1970s was a hotbed of the future titled players of chess. Future Grandmaster Larry Christiansen, future International Masters Perry Youngworth, and

3....Ke7 4. Ke5

BK blocks WP, and WK defends WP

Figure 8.27

4....Ke8 5. Kf6

BK steps back, WK steps to the side

Figure 8.28

5....Kf8 6. e7

BK takes opposition, WP checks

Figure 8.29

6....Ke8 7. Ke6 stalemate

Stalemate

Figure 8.30

Doug Root all played there as preteens and teens. One of the drills the West Covina youngsters practiced was battleship chess.

■ *Materials*

Chess sets, chessboard, barriers. Good barriers include manila file folders, cardboard chessboards, or an opened spiral notebook or three-ring binder.

■ *Procedure*

In this drill, one puts a barrier between the 4th and 5th ranks of the chessboard. The barrier should prevent the opponents from seeing each other's choices during the initial phase of piece and pawn placement. Each player is given one king and four pawns, and places them on the board with the following two restrictions:

1. The white king must be between the 1st and 3rd ranks. The black king must be between the 6th and 8th ranks. That way, when the barrier is lifted, the kings won't be in check from an enemy pawn.
2. The white pawns must be placed between the 2nd and 4th ranks. The black pawns must be placed between the 5th and 7th ranks. Of course, one can't place pawns on the 1st or 8th rank, because pawns never are there.

After both players say they are ready, the barrier is lifted and play begins with white to move. If the players are novices, you can instruct them to play until one person either promotes a pawn or loses all of his pawns. If the players are more advanced, they should keep playing even after one side has promoted a pawn. The side with the promoted pawn (now likely a queen) should try to execute a Q and K vs. K checkmate.

Battleship chess allows students to quickly experiment with many different pawn formations and king positions. Is it better to have all the pawns on the 4th rank, so they are closer to promoting? Is the king better in the center or on a wing? Of what importance are pawn chains or isolated pawns? By repeatedly playing battleship chess, students figure out best placements for kings and pawns. This knowledge makes them better players of chess endgames.

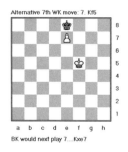

Alternative 7th WK move: 7. Kf5

BK would next play 7....Kxe7

Figure 8.31

A legal starting position for:

Battleship chess

Figure 8.32

Figure 8.32 is an example of a legal starting formation for battleship chess. The photograph (Figure 8.33) shows black making his fourth move from a position that arose out of Figure 8.32. At the close of the lesson, the teacher should have the students discuss what battleship chess formations worked best and why. Generally speaking, the king should be placed in the center, for quick access to both sides of the board. Pawns often work best on the outside files: the a-, b-, g-, and h-files. By having pawns split between the kingside and the queenside of the board, chances are increased to create an outside **passed pawn.** By having outside passed pawns on either wing, the defending king struggles to stop them from promoting.

Figure 8.33

Battleship chess drill being played out.
Copyright 2005 Bob Lindholm.

APPENDIX A

State Standards

In this guide, I demonstrated how including chess could help students meet specific TEKS (Texas Essential Knowledge and Skills). My emphasis on Texas was a result of teaching mostly Texans, on the UT TeleCampus online platform. When converting my online courses to this book, I assumed that the Texas standards would be somewhat similar to those found in other states. In creating this appendix, I've discovered that my assumption was (for the most part) correct. I compared the TEKS I've cited to other states' reading and mathematics standards. When I couldn't find exact matches, I cited related objectives mentioned by other states.

The standards are quotes from the states' education Web sites. Links to the states' Web sites are at the Education World site, http://www.education-world.com, in the Reference Center, Ed Standards link. To make comparisons simpler, the reading TEKS (from my Chapters 4 and 6) are labeled here as A, B, and C, as are the comparable standards from the other states. The word "SOLVE" in the table signals a similar or related reading or mathematics standard to the TEKS problem-solving heuristic, highlighted in chapter 5. In most cases, the SOLVE standard comes from the math framework. When it comes from the reading or language arts framework, I note that as SOLVE (reading). Unless otherwise noted in the left-most column, the standards cited apply to grades K–12.

TEKS cited in Chapter 4

(A) Reading/text structures/literary concepts. The student analyzes the characteristics of various types of texts (genres). The student is expected to:

- identify the purposes of different types of texts, such as to inform, influence, express, or entertain;

- recognize and analyze story plot, setting, and problem resolution (taught in grades 4–8).

(B) Reading/literary response. The student expresses and supports responses to various types of texts. The student is expected to:

- offer observations, make connections, react, speculate, interpret, and raise questions in response to texts;

- connect, compare, and contrast ideas, themes, and issues across text (taught in grades 4–8).

TEKS cited in Chapter 6

(C) Reading/comprehension. The student comprehends selections using a variety of strategies (taught in grades 4–8).

TEKS cited in Chapter 5

SOLVE: Understanding the problem, making a plan, carrying out the plan, evaluating the solution for reasonableness (taught in grades 3–8).

State	Standards
AL, Grades 3–5	(A) Interpret passages in print material, including identifying author's purpose; use literary analysis, including identifying and analyzing setting, and plot, including problem and solution. (B) Compare and contrast story elements and the experiences and feelings of literary characters to students' lives. (C) Use a wide range of strategies to interpret, evaluate, appreciate, and construct meaning from print materials. SOLVE: Develop and strengthen the skills needed to communicate, reason, solve mathematical problems, and reach higher levels of cognitive reasoning.
AK	(A) Reflect on, analyze, and evaluate a variety of oral, written, and visual information and experiences. (B) Relate what the student views, reads, and hears to practical purposes in the student's own life, to the world outside, and to other texts and experiences. (C) A student who meets the content standard should: comprehend meaning from written text and oral and visual information by applying a variety of reading, listening, and viewing strategies. SOLVE: A student should understand and be able to select and use a variety of problem-solving strategies.
AR Grade 4; K–12	(A) Analyze and compare the distinguishing features of familiar genres (4th grade). (B) Listen and respond to literature, including inferring underlying themes or messages (4th grade). (C) Students shall apply a variety of strategies to read and comprehend written materials (all grades K–12). SOLVE: Students shall develop and evaluate inferences and predictions that are based on data.

AZ	(A) This concept addresses the structure and elements of text such as plot, characters, and theme, but also analyze, interpret, conclude, and draw inferences. In this strand, students are expected to identify, analyze, and interpret a variety of genres, relating them to their own experience and knowledge. (B) This concept recognizes that comprehension of literary text is enhanced by an informed awareness of global issues and cultures. Literature that crosses cultural and national boundaries offers an excellent experience for students to broaden their horizons and understanding. (C) Good readers consciously use comprehension strategies to make sense of what they have read. SOLVE: Evaluate situations, select problem-solving strategies, draw logical conclusions, develop and describe solutions, and recognize and describe their applications.
CA Grades 4–8	(A) Find similarities and differences between texts in the treatment, scope, or organization of ideas. (B) Identify and analyze recurring themes across works. (C) Students read and understand grade-level-appropriate material. They draw upon a variety of comprehension strategies as needed. SOLVE: Students move beyond a particular problem by generalizing to other situations: Evaluation of the reasonableness of the solution in the context of the original situation.
CO Grades 5–8	(A) Determining literary quality based on elements such as the author's use of vocabulary, character development, plot development, description of setting, and realism of dialogue. (B) Comparing the diverse voices of our national experience as they read a variety of United States literature. (C) Use a full range of strategies to comprehend. SOLVE: Students who reason mathematically gather data, make conjectures, assemble evidence, and build an argument to support or refute these conjectures.
CT SOLVE (reading) Grades 5–8	(A) & (B) Students will read and respond in individual, literary, critical, and evaluative ways to literary, informational, and persuasive texts. (C) Students will choose and apply strategies that enhance the fluent and proficient use of language arts. SOLVE: Students will predict as they read, listen to and view texts, then review the texts to assess the plausibility of their predictions.
DC Grade 4	(A) The student recognizes story elements in fiction (problem, character, setting, plot, theme, climax); evaluates author's purpose and the techniques the author used to convey the message. (B) The student compares/contrasts texts, poems, and stories. (C) The student adjusts reading rate to match purpose and difficulty of materials. SOLVE: The student generalizes patterns and functional relationships; uses symbolic forms to represent mathematical situations; analyzes change in real and abstract situations; and solves real-life and career-related problems.
DE End of Grade 5; Grades K–10	(A) Students will respond to literary text and media using interpretive, critical, and evaluative processes by recognizing the effect of such literary devices as figurative language, dialogue, and description; understanding the differences between genres (by end of grade 5). (B) Students will use literary knowledge accessed through print and visual media to connect self to society and culture (grades K–10). (C) Students will access, organize, and evaluate information gained by listening, reading, and viewing (grades K–10). SOLVE: Problem solving should emphasize the *process* that could lead to a reasonable solution, not just the solution. Understanding and knowledge are often developed during the process of trying to find solutions (grades K–10).

FL Grades 3–5	(A) The student understands the common features of a variety of literary forms. (B) The student responds critically to fiction, nonfiction, poetry, and drama. (C) The students uses the reading process effectively, select[ing] from a variety of simple strategies. SOLVE: The student describes, analyzes, and generalizes a wide variety of patterns, relations, and functions.
GA Grade 4	(A) Identifies literary forms (e.g., fiction, nonfiction, poetry, and drama). (B) Responds to literal, inferential, and evaluative questions about literature. (C) Reads for understanding and rereads as needed for clarification, self-correction, and further comprehension. SOLVE: Employs problem-solving strategies (e.g., make a chart, graph, or table; make an organized list; guess and check; make a simple problem; look for a pattern; draw a picture; or work backwards).
HI	(A) Students will apply knowledge of the conventions of language and texts to construct meaning. (B) Students will respond to texts from a range of stances: initial understanding, personal, interpretive, critical. (C) Students will use strategies within the reading process to construct meaning. SOLVE: Students should be able to use mathematics as a tool for solving problems they encounter.
IA	Local control of standards.
ID Grade 4	(A) The student will identify defining characteristics of . . . literary forms and genres. (B) The student will read and respond to a variety of literature. (C) Read a variety of grade-level materials and apply strategies appropriate to various situations. SOLVE: The student will understand and use a variety of problem-solving skills.
IL	(A) Understand how literary elements and techniques are used to convey meaning. (B) Read and interpret a variety of literary works. (C) Apply reading strategies to improve understanding and fluency. SOLVE: Students must have experience with a wide variety of problem-solving methods and opportunities for solving a wide range of problems. The ability to link the problem-solving methods learned in mathematics with a knowledge of objects and concepts from other academic areas is a fundamental survival skill for life.
IN	(A) Response to grade-level-appropriate literature includes identifying story elements such as character, theme, plot, and setting, and making connections and comparisons across texts. (B) Literary response enhances students' understanding of history, culture, and the social sciences. (C) Reading comprehension: Students develop strategies such as asking questions; making predictions; and identifying and analyzing structure, organization, perspective, and purpose. SOLVE: Good problem solvers develop a range of strategies for finding solutions to problems and learn to monitor and adjust the strategies they choose in the process of solving a problem.
KS	(A) Learners demonstrate knowledge of literature from a variety of cultures, genres, and time periods. (B) Learners demonstrate skills needed to read and respond to literature. (C) Learners demonstrate skill in reading a variety of materials for a variety of purposes. SOLVE: The student uses algebraic concepts and procedures in a variety of situations.

KY (distinguished level)	(A) Student demonstrates an extensive understanding of literary elements. (B) Student makes insightful connections between their ideas and the text. (C) Student selectively uses strategies such as skimming, scanning, and formulating questions in multiple contexts. SOLVE (reading): Student identifies the problem, selects information, and evaluates the solution.
LA	(A) Students identify (K–4) and classify (5–8) various genres according to their unique characteristics. (B) Students read, analyze, and respond to literature as a record of life experiences. (C) Students read, comprehend, and respond to a range of materials, using a variety of strategies for different purposes. SOLVE: Students should be able to design problems and generate appropriate solutions.
MA	(A) Students will identify, analyze, and apply knowledge of the structure and elements of fiction and provide evidence from the text to support their understanding. (B) Students will identify, analyze, and apply knowledge of theme and provide evidence from the text to support their understanding. (C) Students need to develop a repertoire of learning strategies that they consciously practice and apply in increasingly diverse and demanding contexts. SOLVE: To become good problem solvers, students need many opportunities to formulate questions, model problem situations in a variety of ways, generalize mathematical relationships, and solve problems in both mathematical and everyday contexts.
MD Grades 3–8	(A) Students will use elements of literary text to facilitate understanding. (B) Students will read, comprehend, interpret, analyze, and evaluate literary texts. (C) Students will use a variety of strategies to understand what they read (construct meaning). SOLVE: (a) Identify the question in the problem; (b) Decide if enough information is present to solve the problem; (c) Make a plan to solve a problem; (d) Apply a strategy, i.e., draw a picture, guess and check, finding a pattern, writing an equation; (e) Select a strategy, i.e., draw a picture, guess and check, finding a pattern, writing an equation; (f) Identify alternative ways to solve a problem; (g) Show that a problem might have multiple solutions or no solution; (h) Extend the solution of a problem to a new problem situation.
ME Grades 5–8	(A) Students will recognize the use of specific literary devices [and the] complex elements of plot. (B) Students will identify the universality of themes and examine the connections among various expressive forms. (C) Students will use the skills and strategies of the reading process to comprehend, interpret, evaluate, and appreciate what they have read. SOLVE: People use math skills daily to identify problems, look for information that will help solve the problems, consider a variety of solutions, and communicate the best solution to others.
MI	(A) All students will read and analyze a wide variety of classic and contemporary literature and other texts to seek information, ideas, enjoyment, and understanding, of their individuality, our common heritage and common humanity, and the rich diversity of our society. (B) All students will explore and use the characteristics of different types of texts, aesthetic elements, and meaning—including text structure, figurative and descriptive language, spelling, punctuation, and grammar—to construct and convey meaning. (C) All students will demonstrate, analyze, and reflect upon the skills and processes used to communicate through listening, speaking, viewing, reading, and writing. SOLVE: Mathematical power is the ability to explore, to conjecture, to reason logically and to use a variety of mathematical methods effectively to solve problems.

MN Grade 4	(A) & (B) The student will actively engage in the reading process and read, understand, respond to, analyze, interpret, evaluate, and appreciate a wide variety of fiction, poetic, and nonfiction texts. (C) The student will use a variety of strategies to expand reading, listening, and speaking vocabularies. SOLVE: The student will apply skills of mathematical representation, communication, and reasoning.
MO	(A) Reading and evaluating fiction, poetry and drama. (B) Identifying and evaluating relationships between language and culture. (C) *No comparable standard found.* SOLVE: Students in Missouri public schools will acquire the knowledge and skills to recognize and solve problems.
MS Grade 4	(A) Read, analyze, and respond in written and oral language or other art forms to increasingly challenging literature and other resources. (B) Construct meaning by applying personal experiences and by reading, writing, speaking, listening, and viewing. (C) Read independently with fluency and for meaning using a variety of strategies. SOLVE: Students will be provided with learning experiences that enable them to select appropriate strategies to solve problems in the real world. Through actively investigating and discussing mathematical ideas using a variety of tools, students will have the opportunity to become confident problem solvers.
MT	(A) Students recognize and evaluate how language, literary devices, and elements contribute to the meaning and impact of literary works. (B) Students construct meaning as they comprehend, interpret, analyze and respond to literary works. (C) Students apply a range of skills and strategies to read. SOLVE: Students engage in the mathematical processes of problem solving and reasoning.
NC Grades 3–5	(A) Students need to develop some understanding of the distinguishing features and structures of texts. (B) When students read texts that reflect the diversity of our culture in terms of gender, age, social class, religion, and ethnicity among individuals, they deepen their personal learning. (C) Students need an array of strategies for comprehending, interpreting, evaluating, and appreciating texts they read and texts they compose. SOLVE (reading): Students in modern society must be prepared to apply higher level thinking skills to make decisions and solve problems.
ND Grade 4	(A) Determine the elements of a fiction text; i.e., setting, characters, development, rising action, events, problems, resolution/solution. (B) Compare and contrast characteristics of fiction; compare and contrast texts. (C) Use a variety of text comprehension strategies to improve and monitor understanding. SOLVE: Students will become mathematical problem solvers.
NE Grade 4	(A) Students will identify and use characteristics to classify different types of text. (B) Students will identify similarities and differences between two fourth grade level reading selections. (C) Students will demonstrate the use of multiple strategies in reading. SOLVE: Students will identify, describe, and extend arithmetic patterns.
NH	(A) Recognize and understand story elements including character, setting, conflict, plot, and theme. (B) Students will demonstrate competence in understanding, appreciating, interpreting, and critically analyzing classical and contemporary American and British literature as well as literary works translated into English.

(C) Good readers . . . employ multiple strategies and processes to understand the written word. SOLVE: *All students* will develop strong mathematical problem solving and reasoning abilities [italics in original].

NJ   (A) & (B) Students should read grade-level-appropriate or more challenging classic and contemporary literature. . . . A diversity of material (including fiction and nonfiction) provides students with opportunities to grow intellectually, emotionally, and socially as they consider universal themes, diverse cultures and perspectives, and the common aspects of human existence. (C) Students apply literal, inferential, and critical comprehension strategies before, during, and after reading to examine, construct, and extend meaning. SOLVE: Students posing and solving meaningful problems.

NM   (A) & (B) Students will use literature and media to develop an understanding of people, societies, and the self. (C) Students will apply strategies and skills to comprehend information that is read, heard, and viewed. SOLVE: Students will understand [subject matter within mathematics] through problem solving, reasoning and proof, making connections and representations, and using effective communication.

NV   (A) & (B) Students read to comprehend, interpret, and evaluate literature from a variety of authors, cultures, and times. (C) Students use reading process skills and strategies to build comprehension. SOLVE: Students will develop their ability to solve problems by engaging in developmentally appropriate problem-solving opportunities in which there is a need to use various approaches to investigate and understand mathematical concepts in order to formulate their own problems; find solutions to problems from everyday situations; develop and apply strategies to solve a wide variety of problems; and integrate mathematical reasoning, communication, and connections.

NY   (A) Students will read and listen to oral, written, and electronically produced texts and performances from American and world literature; relate texts and performances to their own lives; and develop an understanding of the diverse social, historical, and cultural dimensions the texts and performances represent. (B) As listeners and readers, students will analyze experiences, ideas, information, and issues presented by others using a variety of established criteria. (C) Students will listen, speak, read, and write for information and understanding. SOLVE: Students will apply the knowledge and thinking skills of mathematics, science, and technology to address real-life problems and make informed decisions.

OH   (A) [Students] demonstrate their comprehension by describing and discussing the elements of literature (e.g., setting, character, and plot), analyzing the author's use of language (e.g., word choice and figurative language), comparing and contrasting texts, inferring theme and meaning, and responding to text in critical and creative ways. (B) Strategic readers learn to explain, analyze, and critique literary text to achieve deep understanding. (C) Students develop and learn to apply strategies that help them to comprehend and interpret informational and literary texts. Reading and learning to read are problem-solving processes that require strategies for the reader to make sense of written language and remain engaged with texts. SOLVE: Students apply problem-solving and decision-making techniques, and communicate mathematical ideas.

OK (SOLVE for Grades 1–5)	(A) & (B) The student will read to construct meaning and respond to a wide variety of literary forms. (C) The student will apply a wide range of strategies to comprehend, interpret, evaluate, appreciate, and respond to a wide variety of texts. SOLVE: Require appropriate reasoning and problem-solving experiences from the outset, instilling in students a sense of confidence in their ability to think and communicate mathematically.
OR	(A) Develop an interpretation of a grade-level literary text. (B) Examine content and structure of a grade-level literary text. (C) Listen to, read, and understand a wide variety of informational and narrative text across the subject areas at school and on own, applying comprehension strategies as needed. SOLVE: Students select, apply, and translate mathematical representations to solve problems; apply and adapt a variety of appropriate strategies to solve problems; monitor and reflect on the process of mathematical problem solving; and accurately solve problems that arise in mathematics and other contexts.
PA Grade 5	(A) Compare the use of literary elements within and among texts including characters, setting, plot, theme, and point of view. (B) Read and respond to nonfiction and fiction including poetry and drama. (C) Identify the basic ideas and facts in text using strategies. SOLVE: Develop a plan to analyze a problem, identify the information needed to solve the problem, carry out the plan, check whether an answer makes sense, and explain how the problem was solved.
RI	(A) All students will know the processes used to construct and convey meaning through text, and will develop and apply criteria for the evaluations and appreciation of their own and others' texts. (B) All students will use themes and topics from text to make connections and demonstrate an understanding of commonalities and diversity through exploration of universal issues. (C) All students will demonstrate the ability to understand and respond to a wide variety of text. SOLVE: Mathematics as problem solving, communication, reasoning, and connections can be considered the processes by which one learns mathematics.
SC	(A) & (B) The students will use knowledge of the purposes, structures, and elements of writing to analyze and interpret various types of text. (C) The student will draw upon a variety of strategies to comprehend, interpret, analyze, and evaluate what he or she reads. SOLVE: Instructional programs from prekindergarten through grade 12 should enable all students to accomplish the following: build new mathematical knowledge through problem solving; solve problems that arise in mathematics and in other contexts; apply and adapt a variety of appropriate strategies to solve problems; and monitor and reflect on the process of mathematical problem solving.
SD	(A) & (B) Students are able to evaluate text structures, literary elements, and literary devices within various genres to develop interpretations and form responses. (C) Students are able to apply various reading strategies to comprehend and interpret text. SOLVE: An understanding of patterns is basic to all mathematical thinking.
TN Grade 4	(A) Read, view, and recognize various literary (e.g., poetry, novels, historical fiction, nonfiction) and media (e.g., photographs, the arts, films, video) genres. (B) Compare and contrast different versions/representations of the same stories/events that reflect different cultures. (C) Use active comprehension strategies to

derive meaning while reading and to check for understanding after reading. SOLVE: Use visualization, spatial reasoning, and geometric modeling to solve problems.

TX Grades 4–8	(A) The student analyzes the characteristics of various types of texts (genres). The student is expected to: identify the purposes of different types of texts, such as to inform, influence, express, or entertain; recognize and analyze story plot, setting, and problem resolution. (B) The student expresses and supports responses to various types of texts. The student is expected to: offer observations, make connections, react, speculate, interpret, and raise questions in response to texts; connect, compare, and contrast ideas, themes, and issues across text. (C) The student comprehends selections using a variety of strategies. SOLVE: Understanding the problem, making a plan, carrying out the plan, evaluating the solution for reasonableness.
UT Grade 4	(A) & (B) Recognize and use features of narrative and informational text. (C) Apply strategies to comprehend text. SOLVE: By the end of fourth grade students will be able to become mathematical problem solvers.
VA Grade 4	(A) & (B) The student will also read classic and contemporary literature selections by a variety of authors. (C) The student will use text organizers, summarize information, formulate questions, and draw conclusions to demonstrate reading comprehension. SOLVE: Problem solving has been integrated throughout the six content strands. The development of problem-solving skills should be a major goal of the mathematics program at every grade level.
VT Grade PreK–8	(A) & (B) In written responses to literature, students show understanding of reading; connect what has been read to the broader world of ideas, concepts, and issues; and make judgments about the text. (C) Students use a variety of strategies to help them read. SOLVE: Students produce solutions to mathematical problems requiring decisions about approach and presentation, so that final drafts are appropriate in terms of these dimensions: Approach & Reasoning—The reasoning, strategies, and skills used to solve the problem; Connections—Demonstration of observations, applications, extensions, and generalizations; Solution—All of the work that was done to solve the problem, including the answer.
WA Grade 4	(A) Understand and analyze story elements. Use knowledge of situation and characters' actions, motivations, feelings, and physical attributes to determine characters' traits. Identify the main events in a plot, including the cause and effect relationship in problem solving. (B) Apply the skills of drawing conclusions, providing a response, and expressing insights to informational/expository text and literary/narrative text. (C) The student understands and uses different skills and strategies to read. SOLVE: The student uses mathematics to define and solve problems. Understand problems. Analyze a situation to define a problem.
WI Grade 4	(A) Read, interpret, and critically analyze literature. Recognize and recall elements and details of story structure, such as sequence of events, character, plot, and setting, in order to reflect on meaning. (B) Read and discuss literary and nonliterary texts in order to understand human experience. Demonstrate the ability to integrate general knowledge about the world and familiarity with literary and nonliterary texts when reflecting upon life's experiences. (C) Use effective reading strategies to achieve their purposes in reading. SOLVE: Students grow in

their ability and persistence in problem solving through extensive classroom experience in posing, formulating, and solving problems at a variety of levels of difficulty and at every level in their mathematical development.

WV Grade 4   (A) Use comprehension skills to understand literary works (e.g., summarize; story elements; skim and scan; define expository text; compare/contrast; imagery; paraphrase; compose personal response; infer; fact and opinion; sequence). (B) Compare self to text in making connections between characters or simple events in a literary work with people and events in one's own and other cultures. (C) Students will use skills to read for literacy experiences, read to inform, and read to perform a task. SOLVE: It is important that all students value mathematics, become confident in their ability to do mathematics, become mathematical problem solvers, communicate mathematically, make connections to other content areas and to the real world application of mathematics, and learn to reason mathematically.

WY   (A) & (B) Literacy skills are applied across a wide range of literary and technical materials, using strategies appropriate to different text types and for different purposes, so students are well prepared to use them in personal interests and professional pursuits. (C) Early mastery of the skills necessary to unlock written language and of the strategies to translate that language into meaningful concepts is essential to success. SOLVE: The development of problem-solving skills should be a major goal of the mathematics program in every strand at every grade level.

APPENDIX B

Chess Worksheets with Answer Keys

Worksheets

This appendix has four worksheets that could be used with the first seven lesson plans in Chapter 8.

The worksheets are titled:

- Algebraic Notation
- Knight Moves
- King Moves and
- Two-Rook Mate

Answer keys for the above worksheets are included at the end of this appendix.

Name _____

Date _____

Algebraic Notation Worksheet

Directions: Under each chess diagram below, write the name of the square with the X on it. Then use the first letters of your answers to spell a word. For example, if your answers were c2, a1, and b3, your word would be cab.

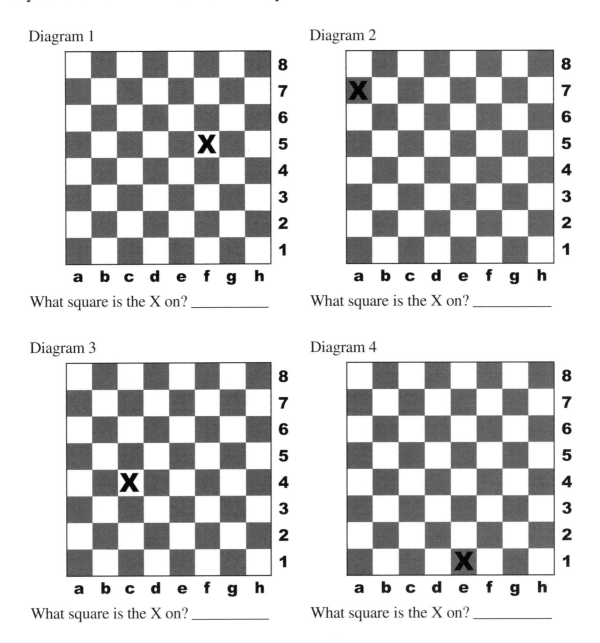

Diagram 1

What square is the X on? _____

Diagram 2

What square is the X on? _____

Diagram 3

What square is the X on? _____

Diagram 4

What square is the X on? _____

What word is spelled by the diagrams? Be sure to put the letter from diagram 1 first, the letter from diagram 2 second, the letter from diagram 3 third, and the letter from diagram 4 fourth.

The four letters of the word are ____ ____ ____ ____

Name_____

Date_____

Knight Moves Worksheet

Directions: Under each chess diagram below, write the names of the squares to which the pictured knight (N) can move. Then, on the back of this paper, explain the chess rule of thumb "a knight on the rim is grim." That is, why are knights worse on the edge of the board than they are in the center?

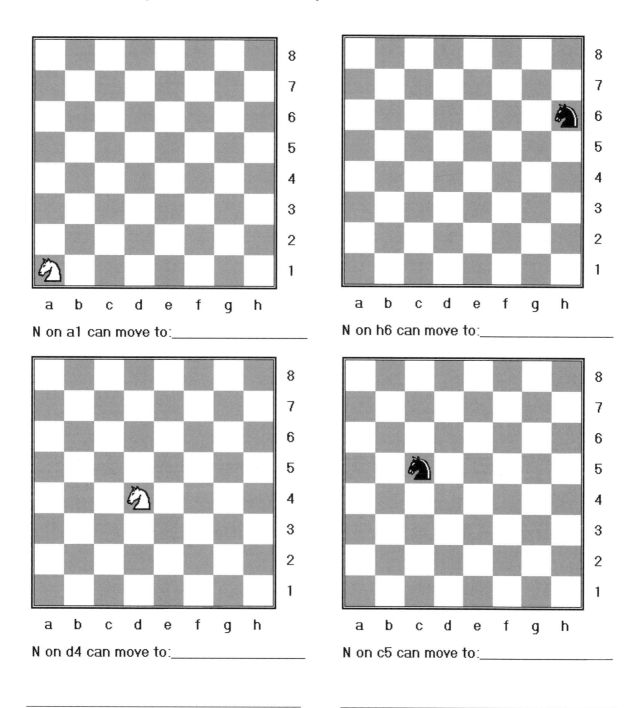

N on a1 can move to:_____

N on h6 can move to:_____

N on d4 can move to:_____

N on c5 can move to:_____

King Moves Worksheet

Directions: A king can move one square in any direction. An attack on a king by an enemy piece or pawn is called a check. The king must get out of check. He can move to a safe square, one where he will not be in check. Or the king can capture the checking piece. Or a friendly piece or a pawn can be used to block the check. In each diagram below, write the next move(s) for the white king (WK) in notation. You can write Ka4 for a king move to a4. You can write Kxa4 if the king captured a piece when he moved to a4.

Black has just played Nb3+

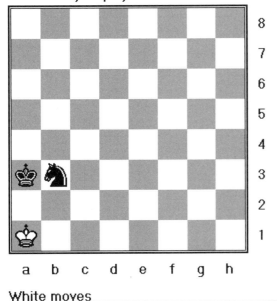

White moves_____

Black has just played Nf5.

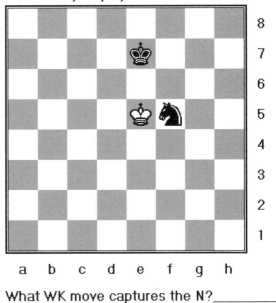

What WK move captures the N?_____

Black has just played Ne5.

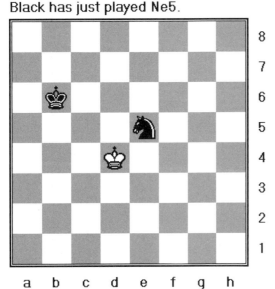

List all possible WK moves_____

Two-Rook Mate Worksheet

Directions: Write the checkmate move for each position in the space provided under the diagram. A checkmate is when you put a king into check and that king cannot escape from check. When every possible move would still leave the attacked king in check, that king is checkmated. In notation, Ra1# means Rook to a1 square checkmate.

Diagram 1. White to move.

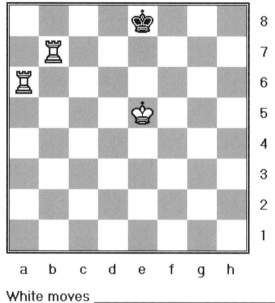

White moves _____

Diagram 2. Black to move.

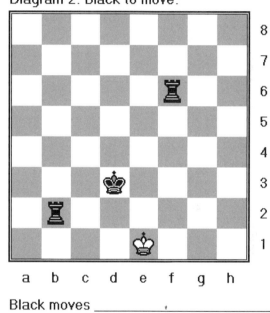

Black moves _____

Diagram 3. White to move.

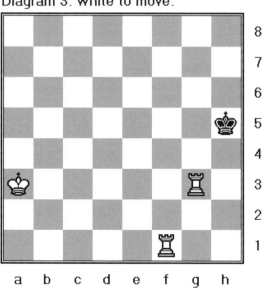

White moves _____

Diagram 4. Black to move.

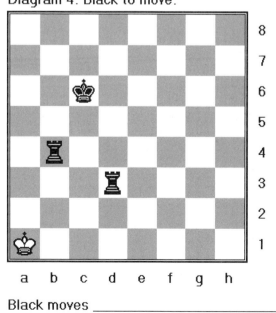

Black moves _____

Answer Keys for Worksheets

Answer key for Algebraic Notation worksheet: Diagram 1 is f5; Diagram 2 is a7; Diagram 3 is c4; Diagram 4 is e1. The four letters form the word **face**.

Answer key for Knight Moves worksheet: N on a1 can move to c2 and b3; N on h6 can move to g4, f5, f7, and g8; N on d4 can move to c2, b3, b5, c6, e6, f5, f3, and e2; N on c5 can move to a6, b7, d7, e6, e4, d3, b3, a4. The student's explanation on the back of the paper should be along the lines of, "Knights on the rim are grim because on the edge of the board they can only move to 2–4 squares. The Na1 could move to 2 squares, the N on h6 to 4 squares. But Ns in or near the center of the board can move to 8 squares. They have more mobility and more control in the middle."

Answer key for King Moves worksheet: For the problem titled, "Black has just played Nb3+," the only legal move by the white king (WK) is Kb1. Reasons: Kb2 or Ka2 puts the WK in check by the black king. For the second question, about which WK move captures the N, the answer is Kxf5. In the third diagram, the WK may move to c3, e3, e4, d5, or play Kxe5. The WK cannot move to c5 because that square is controlled by the BK. The WK cannot move to d3 or c4 because those squares are under the control of the black knight.

Answer key for Two-Rook Mate worksheet: Diagram 1 is Ra8#; Diagram 2 is Rb1#; Diagram 3 is Rh1#; and Diagram 4 Ra3#.

Glossary

Academic curriculum aids students in learning particular subject matters. Students are also introduced to the questions that drive each discipline, and they learn discipline relevant vocabulary and concepts.

Bishop (B) is a chess piece that moves diagonally along unoccupied squares. It can capture an enemy man that is in its path. At the beginning of a game, each player has a light-squared bishop and a dark-squared bishop. A bishop is worth a little more than three pawns, according to most sources.

Blindfold chess is chess played without sight of the board. Each move is called out to the player in notation, and the player responds in notation with the move he or she wants to make next.

Calibrate means to determine the caliber or worth of a person or thing. In the case of Horgan's (1992) research, calibrating means to successfully predict the outcome of chess games based on accurate assessment of one's own and others' abilities at chess.

Castle is a move notated 0-0 (kingside castling) or 0-0-0 (queenside castling). Castling can be done once per side, per game, if the king and rook that want to castle with each other haven't moved previously and the king is not in check, doesn't have to cross over a checked square, and doesn't end up on a checked square. Also, there can be no pieces between the king and rook when castling occurs. To castle, the king moves two squares toward its rook, and the rook hops over the king and lands on the horizontally adjacent square to the king.

Check (+) is an attack on a king by an enemy piece or pawn. The king in check must get out of check by capturing the checking piece or pawn, blocking the check with one of his own men, or moving to a square that is not attacked.

Checkmate (++ or #; also called "mate") occurs when the king is in check and cannot escape from check. Being checkmated means that one has lost the chess game.

Chess diagram is a two-dimensional representation of a chess position. One can make diagrams by hand, by abbreviating the chessmen's names (K, Q, R, B, N, and P) and circling the black chess men. Or one can use a software program such as Chess Captor (http://www.chesscaptor.com), which includes fonts that give figurine representations of white and black pieces.

Chess problem is a chess position (usually represented on a diagram) for which there is a specified solution. For example, a problem might state, "White to move and mate in three." The person studying the problem would either set up the diagrammed position on a chess board and figure out the three moves or solve the problem mentally.

Chess rating is a number assigned to a player based on his or her performance against other rated players. In the USCF, ratings range from the low 100s to around 2800, with a mean of 1500.

Clocks are used to time chess games. One's time runs when it is one's move. At the completion of one's move, one punches a button to start one's opponent's clock running. Some games are sudden death (SD) time controls. That is, one must finish one's whole game before the time elapses. Common SD time controls include G/5 (5 minutes per side for the game, known as speed chess) and G/30. In contrast, some tournaments use such traditional time controls as 40/2, 20/1, 20/1. That translates to "make 40 moves before your first two hours elapse, then make 20 moves per hour for the next two time controls." For both SD and traditional time controls, a loss on time (or "flag fall") means a loss of the game, except when the side claiming a win on time doesn't have sufficient material to deliver a checkmate (e.g., has only a K and B, or has only a K and N).

Demonstration board is a board that hangs on the wall (from a nail or map hook, for example) or from an easel. It is a large version of a chessboard and pieces, and is used for showing chess moves to groups of students. One can order demonstration boards from most chess retailers, including USCF.

Domain "is an organized set of activities within a culture, one typically characterized by a specific symbol system and its attendant operations. Any cultural activity in which individuals participate on more than a casual basis, and in which degrees of expertise can be identified and nurtured, should be considered a domain. Thus physics, cooking, chess, constitutional law, and rap music are all domains in contemporary Western culture" (Gardner, 1999, pp. 82–83).

Draw. As Eade (2005, p. 321) wrote, there are several ways for a draw to result: "(a) by agreement of both players, (b) by stalemate, (c) by the declaration and proof of one player that the same position has appeared three times (with the same player to move), (d) by the declaration and proof of one player that there have been 50 moves during which no piece has been taken and no pawns have been moved, although there are some exceptions to the 50 move rule." In some cases, tournament directors may rule games as drawn. For example, if one's opponent runs out of time (see **Clock**)—but one doesn't have sufficient material to checkmate—a draw is declared. A draw is scored as a half point.

En passant is French for "in passing." The en passant capture can be executed by a pawn that is on one's own fifth rank (i.e., rank 5 for white pawns, rank 4 for black pawns) when an enemy pawn does a double jump to the square adjacent to it. Then the fifth-rank pawn can capture the enemy pawn as if it had moved only one square. The en passant capture is optional, and if chosen must be done on the half-move immediately following the enemy pawn's double jump.

Endgame is the stage of the game where there are few chess pieces and pawns left on the board. Often the king becomes active, attacking enemy pawns and supporting his own pawn's promotion. Endgames can also be called "endings."

Expert chess rating means a USCF rating between 2000 and 2200 points. The mean USCF rating is 1500.

Expertise is not the same as general competence: "There is little evidence that a person highly skilled in one domain can transfer the skill to another" (Chi, Glaser, & Farr, 1988, p. xvii). Expertise is therefore defined by many cognitive scientists as mastery of a particular domain. For chess, expertise is based in visuospatial pattern recognition.

Fédération International des Échecs (FIDE) (Web site http://www.fide.com) is the World Chess Federation with 161 member nations. It maintains a rating system, awards international titles (GM, IM, etc.), and has organized world championships.

File is a vertical column on the chessboard. There are 8 files, labeled a, b, c, d, e, f, g, and h.

Flow occurs when a person concentrates deeply on the activity at hand. During such optimal and enjoyable experiences, the person forgets his worries and may even lose track of time. Mihaly Csikszentmihalyi is the authority on flow and the originator of many research studies on the flow phenomenon.

Forks are attacks on two or more enemy chess pawns or pieces at the same time.

Grandmaster (GM) is an international title awarded by FIDE to players who perform above a predetermined level (usually above 2500 FIDE rating) at tournaments with other titled players. Usually it takes three such performances (three norms) to get the GM title.

Heuristics are problem solving strategies, specifically rules of thumb derived by experience. One uses heuristics when there isn't a pre-established formula or algorithm for solving a problem. An example of a heuristic frequently cited in this guide is "Understand the problem, make a plan, carry out the plan, and evaluate the solution for reasonableness."

Humanistic curriculum is concerned with the self-actualization of students. That is, humanistic curriculum goals help students discover who they are, what they are feeling, what they are striving for, and what is important to them.

Intelligence (general) is defined by many psychometricians as a measurable, general, and largely inherited "property distributed within the general population along a bell-shaped curve" (Gardner, 1999, pp. 7–8).

International Master (IM) is a title awarded by FIDE to players who have performed at a specified level (usually above 2400 FIDE rating) at three international tournaments with other titled players.

King (K) is able to move one square in any direction. The king captures the same way that it moves. The king has a special move, castling (when it moves two squares toward the rook with which it wants to castle). The king must not move into check. If the king is put in check, he must get out of check on the next move. When the king is checkmated or stalemated, the game is over.

Knight (N) is the piece that looks (on most chess sets) like a horse. Like a horse, it can jump over pieces and pawns. The knight's move is in the shape of capital L. Alternatively, the knight's move can be described as two squares horizontally followed by one square vertically, or two squares vertically followed by one square horizontally. It can capture an enemy piece only if it lands on the square of that piece. The knight is generally said to be worth three pawns.

Knight's tour is a chess problem in which a knight is placed on any square on the board and must then (moving as a knight) touch each of the remaining 63 squares once and only once. "The Knight's Tour—An Extremely Simple Solution" Web site is http://www.borderschess.org/KTsimple.htm. Contact Dan Thomasson (DTHOMASSON@carolina.rr.com) for more information.

Locus of control is a psychological concept referring to the degree of control a person believes he has over his life. An internal locus of control means that a person believes that he can influence the course of events; and an external locus of control means that a person believes himself to be largely at the mercy of fate.

Loss in a game can occur because of checkmate, a loss on time (see **Clock**), or because of resigning. A loss is scored as a zero.

Master means a USCF rating between 2200 and 2400. Ratings above 2400 are senior masters, and many players in that rating range also have FIDE titles.

Mate is short for **checkmate**.

Mind's eye "is the meeting point where visual information from the external world is combined and coordinated with visual representations stored in short-term and long-term memory" (Chase & Simon, 1973, p. 277).

Mobility is the ability to move to different parts of the board. One can talk about the mobility of particular pieces and pawns in different positions— for example, a bishop has more mobility than a knight when there are lots of open diagonals, but a knight may have more mobility than a bishop if diagonals are blocked by pawn chains.

Move in chess refers to either making a move (i.e., half of a move pair) for one side, or to the combined white and black move pair. Thus, when a chess problem reads, "white to move" it is white's turn. But when the problem states, "white mates in three moves," that means three white moves (with the required black moves also played): a white move and black move, a second white move and black move, and a third white move completing the mate.

Multiple intelligences (MI) theory was Gardner's break from the psychometric concept of intelligence. Gardner posits eight intelligences that have met his criteria. (More intelligences may be added, if each new intelligence meets the criteria.) The eight intelligences are linguistic, logical-mathematical, musical, bodily-kinesthetic, spatial, interpersonal, intrapersonal, and naturalist (see Figure G.1, graphic courtesy of David Lazear, http://www.multi-intell.com/).

Notation is the writing down of chess moves. The most common notation system today is algebraic notation. Each square has a name based on its file and rank

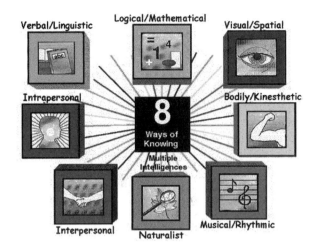

Figure G.1

Eight multiple intelligences.

coordinates. An older system of notation is descriptive notation, which is based on the names and squares that pieces occupy at the beginning of the game: for example, 1. Kt.-KB3 means knight to king's bishop's three. In algebraic, that same move would be written 1. Nf3, meaning knight to the f-file, 3rd rank.

Opening refers to the first 10 or so moves of a chess game, during which time players develop most or all of their pieces. The opening is followed by the middlegame, which is followed by the endgame.

Opposition is when two kings are on the same rank, file, or diagonal with one empty square between them. A player is said to "have the opposition" if his opponent must move, allowing the advance of the player's king along the rank, file, or diagonal. Distant opposition (when there are a greater number of odd squares, such as 3 or 5, between kings) can also be calculated.

Organizing elements are the themes, concepts, generalizations, skills, or philosophical values that ground curricula. Some examples of organizing elements in this book are competition and problem solving. John D. McNeil's *Contemporary Curriculum* (2006) explains organizing elements in detail.

Pairing rules and pairing sheets are features of chess tournaments. Pairing rules ensure that each tournament participant has a roughly equal number of whites and blacks over the course of the event. Pairing sheets tell participants at the start of each tournament round whom to play and with what color (white or black). At the conclusion of each tournament game, participants are responsible for marking results (win, loss, or draw) on the pairing sheet. The tournament director transfers the pairing sheet results onto the **wall chart** after all games in a round are complete.

Passed pawn is a pawn that has no enemy pawn opposing it on its own file or any immediately adjacent file.

Pawn chain is a diagonal set of two or more pawns that protect each other.

Pawns (P) are the smallest units on the chessboard. They move forward, but capture diagonally. A pawn may move one or two squares on its initial move. When it reaches its 8th rank, it can be promoted. See also **en passant**, a special rule for pawn captures.

Pieces are not pawns; they include kings, queens, rooks, bishops, and knights.

Pins happen when a higher value piece is shielded from an enemy queen, rook, or bishop by its own lower value pawn or piece. The lower value pawn or piece is pinned if, when it moves, the higher value piece could be captured by the enemy. For example, an enemy bishop could pin a knight to his own queen. If the knight moved off the bishop's diagonal, the enemy bishop could take the queen. The previous example is a relative pin, because the knight could legally move. An absolute pin occurs when the higher value piece is the king. In that case, the pinned piece is not allowed to move, because the king would then be illegally exposed to check.

Points Players consider points (the number of pawns a piece is worth) as a guide for the fair exchange of pieces. That is, just as one wouldn't want to trade $9 for $3, one would usually refuse to trade a Q (9 points) for an N (3 points). Points can also refer to a player's score in a tournament; that is, "He has one point" means that he either won one game or drew two games. Points can also refer to chess rating, as in "Alexey Root's current USCF rating is 2003, which is many points lower than her peak rating of 2262."

Postmortem is conducted after a chess game is completed. The participants in the game discuss their moves, sometimes joined by interested observers.

Promotion occurs when a pawn reaches its 8th rank and can then be exchanged for an N, B, R, or Q. One usually queens a pawn, as a queen is the piece worth the most points.

Queen (Q) is worth about nine pawns, according to most sources. On any given move, she can choose to move like a rook or like a bishop.

Queening is moving a pawn to its 8th rank (the promotion square) and requesting a queen.

Rank is any horizontal row on a chessboard. There are 8 ranks, labeled 1, 2, 3, 4, 5, 6, 7, and 8 in algebraic notation.

Rook (R) is a chess piece that moves horizontally and vertically, as many squares as are not blocked by its own pieces. It can capture an enemy piece or pawn that is in its path. The rook is usually said to be worth five pawns.

Round robin pairings mean that each player plays every other player in the tournament one time. Colors are determined by a chart, and each player ends up with roughly equal numbers of whites and blacks during the course of the tournament. In a double round robin, each player plays every other player twice: once with white, and once with black.

Scholar's mate is a fast mate for white, because black fails to defend the f7 square. Many beginning chess players fall into the Scholar's mate: 1. e4 e5, 2. Bc4 Bc5, 3. Qh5 Nf6, 4. Qxf7++.

Score sheet contains the notation for a chess game, as written by one of that game's participants.

Simultaneous exhibition (or "simul" for short) is when a single strong chess player plays several people all at the same time. "Numerous boards are set up, in a circle or rectangle, and the single player stands inside this area, moving from board to board, usually playing a single move at a time" (Eade, 2005, p. 336).

Smothered mate is a checkmate where the king is unable to move out of check because all of his possible escape squares are occupied by his own chessmen.

Social adaptationist curriculum is developed in response to social needs, such as AIDS education or anti-drug programs. Students are given information and prescriptions for handling particular situations. Whereas students are asked to look critically at society in social reconstructionist curriculum, in adaptationist curriculum they learn to deal with current problems.

Social reconstructionist curriculum acts for change in schools and society. Upper elementary students often work in groups to design ideal or utopian institutions (hospitals, schools, cities, etc). Older grades participate in community projects, often developing solutions to problems (e.g., foreign language students might provide translation services to immigrants).

Speed chess is a game played with a sudden death time control (see **Clock**). A usual speed chess time control is G/5 (5 minutes per player, per game).

Square of the pawn is an imaginary square shape, one side of which is the number of chessboard squares from the pawn's current location to its queening or promotion square. If the enemy king is able to enter the square (at its border or inside), then it will be able to capture the pawn either before it queens or on its queening move.

Stalemate is when a king is not in check but there are no legal moves for his side. It is scored as a draw.

Swiss system tournaments pair participants with like scores each round. Also, participants never play the same person twice during a Swiss event. By the last round of a Swiss system, players who have won all their games are paired to determine the tournament champion, players who have won about half their games play each other, and players who have lost every game are paired as well. In other words, no one is eliminated after losses in early rounds.

Systemic curriculum "aligns goals, standards, programs, and instructional materials with tests for assessing the outcomes. A measured curriculum reveals whether the school and its teachers are advancing the learning of all and whether diverse groups are acquiring prespecified knowledge and skills" (McNeil, 2006, p. 1).

Touch move means that if one touches a piece or pawn, one has to move it. And if a player touches one of his opponent's chessmen, he must capture it if such a capture is a legal move. If no legal moves are possible with the touched piece, the player can make any other legal move. To disable the touch move rule, simply announce "I adjust" (or "J'adoube") before touching a chessman.

Tournaments are chess contests among more than two players. Some types of tournaments are Swiss system and round robin. Tournaments have rules about time controls (see **Clock**s), pairings, and behavior (one can't get chess advice during games). The tournament director is the official in charge of the tournament.

Tournament directors (TDs) run tournaments according to the rules of chess, either the USCF rules or the FIDE rules.

United States Chess Federation (USCF) (main Web site http://www. uschess.org; sales Web site http://www.uscfsales.com/) is the official governing body for chess in the United States. It also runs the USCF rating system, which ranks member players, and produces a monthly magazine (*Chess Life*).

Wall charts track the round by round scores of tournament participants in a cumulative fashion. That is, if one wins the first round, a "1" is recorded on the wall chart. If one then loses the second round, the "1" is carried over into the round 2 column. So a wall chart for round 2 will show players with

2 (two wins), 1.5 (one win and one draw), 1 (two draws, or one win and one loss), .5 (one draw and one loss), or 0 (two losses).

Wins in chess occur when one player checkmates the other player, or when that player's opponent resigns (gives up) or loses on time (see **Clock**). A win is scored as one point for the winning player.

Resources and References

Resources

Children and Chess: A Guide for Educators touches on a great deal of chess information. What follows is an annotated list of resources, grouped by topic, for use with your students or for your own further study.

Rules of Chess and Beginning Chess Strategies

A number of books and software products can teach all the rules of chess and basic strategies. *Chess Rules for Students* (for complete beginners), *Checkmate! Ideas for Students* (for students who already know chess rules and notation), and *Chess Tactics for Students* (for intermediate students), all by John A. Bain (http://www.chessforstudents.com/), have reproducible chess problem worksheets and answer keys. *Pawn & Queen and In Between,* edited by Frank Elley and available from USCF sales (http://www.uscfsales.com/), covers the rules of chess, includes entertaining stories, and can be ordered with a set of student workbooks. Chess students that already know how to checkmate would benefit from the worksheets in Al Woolum's *The Chess Tactics Workbook*, available at http://www.mychessstore.com/.

Two widely available children's chess books explain the rules of chess and could be adapted to classroom use:

- Nottingham, T., Wade, B., & Lawrence, A. (1993). *Chess for children.* New York: Sterling Publishing. This book contains diagrams and photos of chess positions, stories about chess players, and fiction about the roles of the pawns and pieces.
- Kidder, H. (1990). *The kids' book of chess.* New York: Workman Publishing. This book features beautiful illustrations and tells the medieval history behind each of the chess figures.

I recommend the software used in my course, Think Like a King® School Chess Software System. That complete system for teaching chess, organizing a school chess club, and pairing tournaments is available at http://www.schoolchess.com. The Think Like a King® School Chess Software System starts with beginner lessons (*Your First Lessons in Chess©*), but its other CDs cover advanced chess topics. The book *Chess for Dummies* (2005) similarly begins at the beginning, but ends with illustrative games that even chess masters benefit from studying.

My husband, International Master Doug Root, listed the following books as his top picks for beginning chess players. Doug's descriptions follow each book title.

- Fred Reinfeld, *1001 Winning Chess Sacrifices and Combinations:* a collection of problems grouped into thematic categories and organized into levels of increasing difficulty.
- Fischer, Margulies, and Mosenfelder, *Bobby Fischer Teaches Chess:* rules and beginning principles to chess play with a chess diagram per page format.
- Aron Nimzowitsch, *My System:* in depth discussion of themes in chess play.
- Hans Kmoch, *Pawn Power in Chess:* a survey of the elements of pawn play.
- Paul Keres, *Practical Chess Endings:* well annotated endgame studies covering the major common endgame positions.

Chess in Education Foundations

Several nonprofits sponsor chess instruction in schools, develop chess curricula, or hold scholastic tournaments. What follows is an alphabetical listing of some of the more established, currently active, large organizations; no endorsement is intended. Most of these organizations operate primarily on the West or East coast.

- American Chess School, http://www.amchess.org/
- America's Foundation for Chess, http://www.af4c.org/
- Berkeley Chess School, http://www.berkeleychessschool.org/
- Chess for Success, http://www.chessforsuccess.org/
- Chess-in-the-Schools, http://www.chessintheschools.org/

- Chess Mates Foundation, http://www.chessmates.org/
- Kasparov Chess Foundation, http://kasparovchessfoundation.org/
- National Scholastic Chess Foundation, http://www.nscfchess.org/
- Success Chess Schools, http://www.successchess.com/

If you live in the middle of the United States, or in a smaller community, visit the State Affiliates Directory Web site, found under "Links" at the USCF Web site (http://www.uschess.org/).

Chess Effectiveness Studies

One of the USCF's slogans is "Chess Makes You Smart." Reports to support that claim are available through the USCF, home page http://www.uschess.org, 1-800-388-KING. Ordering information for research studies is at http://www.uschess.org/scholastic/sc-research.html. Note that the USCF has moved from its former New York headquarters, so the ordering address for research studies is now US Chess, PO Box 3967, Crossville, TN 38557. The USCF also sponsors several committees concerned with topics of interest to educators. The scholastic chess committee, the college chess committee, and the chess in education committee can all be contacted through USCF's home page.

Chess Politics, Ratings, and Tournaments

The politics of chess is discussed in *New in Chess,* http://www.newinchess.com, which also covers grandmaster chess games. Books on the world of chess politics include (1) *ChessDon,* Don Schultz, ChessDon Publishing, 1999, ordering information at http://www.chessdon.com and (2) *Queen of the Kings Game,* Zsuza Polgar and Jacob Shutzman, CompChess, New York, 1997, ordering information at http://www.polgarchess.com. At http://groups.google.com, there is the recreation usenet newsgroup rec.games.chess.politics. This Google group has postings on such topics as whether chess players should undergo drug testing, the relocation of the USCF headquarters, the quality of the national magazine *Chess Life*, why scholastic USCF members often don't renew their memberships, and how USCF could benefit from the Internet chess–playing boom. Interesting posts must be located among the many other posts that could be called flames or spam.

Technical information about the rating system and tournaments is available from USCF, http://www.uschess.org/ratings/. For theoretical information by the developer of the modern rating system, see Elo, A. (1978). *The rating of chessplayers, past and present.* New York: Arco.

Computer Chess, Internet Chess, and Web Sites Cited

Computer chess programs now include high-level strategies, like those employed by human players, in addition to their traditionally formidable brute force calculation powers. How computers' high-level strategies might make them more helpful as chess tutors is discussed in Lazzeri, S. G., & Heller, R. (1996). An intelligent consultant system for chess. *Computers & Education, 27*(3/4), 181–196. Whether a computer defeating the world chess champion makes chess obsolete for humans is discussed in Hope, L. (1994, March). Mission possible: Computers in chess and a-level mathematics. *The Mathematical Gazette, 78* (481), 11–17.

On the World Wide Web, one can play chess with other people and with chess computers. Most servers have settings to filter out chat from guests and chat that contains obscenities. Nevertheless, parents and teachers should monitor the chat that accompanies chess games on servers. The biggest chess server is the Internet Chess Club, http://www.chessclub.com. Membership discounts are available for students. Free Internet Chess Server (FICS) is free for all chess players, and is located at http://www.freechess.org. Finally, many multipurpose servers (e.g., Yahoo! and MSN) have chess games.

Web sites mentioned in the introduction and Chapters 1–8, in order of appearance, are (a) Texas Essential Knowledge and Skills, http://www.tea.state.tx.us; (b) UT TeleCampus, http://www.telecampus.utsystem.edu; (c) United States Chess Federation (USCF) book and equipment sales, http://www.uscfsales.com/; (d) Chess-in-the-Schools (New York), http://www.chessintheschools.org; (e) FIDE (World Chess Federation), http://www.fide.com; (f) Susan Polgar (women's chess champion and girls' tournament founder), http://www.polgarchess.com; (g) John Buky, http://www.thechessacademy.org; (h) Chess House (source for books and equipment, including the book *Chess Poems*), http://www.chesshouse.com/; (i) Chess Captor (diagram software), http://www.chesscaptor.com; and (j) science classification Web sites listed in Josh Eaton's lesson plan: http://www.factmonster.com; http://falcon.jmu.edu/~ramseyil/vertebrates.htm; and http://www.fi.edu/tfi/units/life/classify/classify.html.

Chess Camps

Some of the photos in this book were taken at the Karpov Chess School in Lindsborg, KS (http://www.intecsus.org/intecs/index.html) and the Hummingbird Chess Camp in Jemez Springs, NM (http://www.hummingbirdmusiccamp.org). At those camps, in the summer of 2005, I tested lesson plans from this book. I've also developed chess instructional ideas at the Klein Chess Camp in Spring, TX, run by Jim Liptrap (http://jliptrap.us/).

Chess camps are best suited for children ages 8 and older, though some 6- or 7-year-olds with long attention spans might also like camp. Some camps have adult chess classes. Others feature continuing education workshops for teachers interested in chess-teaching strategies. Almost all camps group students according to a combination of age and chess ability. Most camps have a range from novice to 1500-rated USCF chess player—an average adult rating, but a fairly high rating for a child or young teenager. When I taught in 2005, my children came along as chess campers. William was 8 and a half, and Clarissa was 12. They and I thoroughly enjoyed the Kansas, New Mexico, and Texas chess experiences. To find chess camps in your area, contact the USCF.

References

Books

Buchwald, A. (1993). *Leaving home: A memoir.* New York: G.P. Putnam's Sons.

Carroll, L. (1997). *Alice's adventures in wonderland and through the looking-glass.* Penguin, UK: Puffin. (Combined volume first published in Puffin Books 1962; original *Through the looking-glass* published 1871)

Chase, W. G., & Simon, H. A. (1973). The mind's eye in chess. In W. G. Chase (Ed.), *Visual information processing* (pp. 215–281). New York: Academic Press.

Chi, M. T. H., Glaser, R., & Farr, M. J. (Eds.). (1988). *The nature of expertise.* Hillsdale, NJ: Lawrence Erlbaum.

Coles, R. (1997). *The moral intelligence of children.* New York: Random House.

Cranberg, L. D., & Albert, M. L. (1988). The chess mind. In L. K. Obler & D. Fein (Eds.), *The exceptional brain: Neuropsychology of talent and special abilities* (pp. 156–190). New York: Guilford Press.

Csikszentmihalyi, M. (1990). *Flow: The psychology of optimal experience.* New York: HarperCollins.

Csikszentmihalyi, M. (1996). *Creativity: Flow and the psychology of discovery and invention.* New York: HarperCollins.

de Groot, A. D. (1966). Perception and memory versus thought: Some old ideas and recent findings. In B. Kleinmuntz (Ed.), *Problem solving: Research, method, and theory* (pp. 19–50). New York: Krieger.

Eade, J. (2005). *Chess for dummies* (2nd ed.). New York: Wiley.

Engh, F. (1999). *Why Johnny hates sports.* New York: Avery.

Franklin, B. (1987). The morals of chess. In J. A. L. Lemay (Ed.), *Selections* (pp. 927–931). New York: Viking. (Original work published 1779)

Gardner, H. (1999). *Intelligence reframed: Multiple intelligences for the 21st century.* New York: Basic Books.

Harmin, M. (1990). *How to plan a program for moral education.* Alexandria, VA: Association for Supervision and Curriculum Development.

Hochberg, B. (Ed.). (1993). *The 64-square looking glass: The great game of chess in world literature.* New York: Times Books.

Krogius, N. (1976). *Psychology in chess.* New York: RHM.

Magill, R. A., Ash, M. J., & Smoll, F. L. (Eds.). (1982). *Children in sport* (2nd ed.). Champaign, IL: Human Kinetics.

Martens, R. (1982). Kid sports: A den of iniquity or land of promise. In R. A. Magill, M. J. Ash, & F. L. Smoll (Eds.), *Children in sport* (2nd ed., pp. 204–218). Champaign, IL: Human Kinetics.

Maslow, A. (1968). *Toward a psychology of being* (2nd ed.). New York: Van Nostrand Reinhold.

May, R. (1975). *The courage to create.* New York: W.W. Norton.

McNeil, J. D. (2006). *Contemporary curriculum in thought and action* (6th ed.). New York: John Wiley & Sons.

Moreno, F. (2002). *Teaching life skills through chess: A guide for educators and counselors.* Baltimore: American Literary Press.

Oliner, S. P., & Oliner, P. M. (1988). *The altruistic personality: Rescuers of Jews in Nazi Europe.* New York: Free Press.

Pandolfini, B. (2003). *Every move must have a purpose: Strategies from chess for business and life.* New York: Hyperion.

Passer, M. W. (1982). Psychological stress in youth sports. In R. A. Magill, M. J. Ash, & F. L. Smoll (Eds.), *Children in sport* (2nd ed., pp. 153–177). Champaign, IL: Human Kinetics.

Pelts, R. & Alburt, L. (1992). *Comprehensive chess course* (3rd ed., Vols. I–II). New York: Chess Information and Research Center.

Polya, G. (1957). *How to solve it: A new aspect of mathematical method* (2nd ed.). Princeton: Princeton University Press.

Rowling, J. K. (1997). *Harry Potter and the sorcerer's stone.* New York: Scholastic.

Smith, R. E., & Smoll, F. L. (1982). Psychological stress: A conceptual model and some intervention strategies in youth sports. In R. A. Magill, M. J. Ash, & F. L. Smoll (Eds.), *Children in sport* (2nd ed., pp. 178–195). Champaign, IL: Human Kinetics.

Sullivan, M. (2003). *Connecting boys with books: What libraries can do.* Chicago: American Library Association.

Taylor, A. L. (1979). *The white knight: A study of C. L. Dodgson (Lewis Carroll).* Edinburgh: The Arden Library. (Original work published 1952)

Winner, E. (1996). *Gifted children: Myths and realities.* New York: Basic Books.

Journal Articles

Charness, N. (1981). Aging and skilled problem solving. *Journal of Experimental Psychology: General, 110* (1), 21–38.

Charness, N., & Gerchak, Y. (1996, January). Participation rates and maximal performance: A log-linear explanation for group differences, such as Russian and male dominance in chess. *Psychological Science, 7* (1), 46–51.

Flora, Carlin (2005, July/August). The Grandmaster Experiment. *Psychology Today, 38* (4), 75–84.

Frydman, M., & Lynn, R. (1992). The general intelligence and spatial abilities of gifted young Belgian chess players. *British Journal of Psychology, 83,* 233–235.

Galitis, I. (2002). Stalemate: Girls and a mixed-gender chess club. *Gender and Education, 14* (1), 71–83.

Gobet, F., & Simon, H. A. (1996). Templates in chess memory: A mechanism for recalling several boards. *Cognitive Psychology, 31,* 1–40.

Gurin, P., Gurin, G., & Morrison, B. M. (1978). Personal and ideological aspects of internal and external control. *Social Psychology 41* (4), 275–296.

Horgan, D. D. (1992). Children and chess expertise: The role of calibration. *Psychological Research, 54,* 44–50.

Horgan, D. D., & Morgan, D. (1990). Chess expertise in children. *Applied Cognitive Psychology, 4,* 109–128.

Humble, P. N. (1998, summer). Marcel Duchamp: Chess aesthete and anartist unreconciled. *Journal of Aesthetic Education, 32* (2), 41–55.

Kriz, M., Vokal, E., & Krizova, M. (1990, November). The impact of psychological stress on somatic and biochemical parameters in an atypical sports discipline [translation of Slovak title], *Ceskoslovenske Zdravotnictvii, 38* (11), 479–485.

Lever, J. (1976, April). Sex differences in the games children play. *Social Problems, 23,* 478–487.

Schultetus, R. S., & Charness, N. (1999). Recall or evaluation of chess positions revisited: The relationship between memory and evaluation in chess skill. *American Journal of Psychology, 112* (4), 555–569.

Yoskowitz, J. (1991). Chess versus quasi-chess: The role of knowledge of legal rules. *The American Journal of Psychology, 104* (3), 355–366.

Documents, Downloaded Articles, Magazine and Newspaper Articles, Unpublished Papers

Barber, D. (2003). *A guide to scholastic chess.* Retrieved June 22, 2005, from http://www.amchesseq.com/Guide/2003SCguide.pdf.

Beutler, P. (1995, June 17). The new chess set. *Lincoln Journal-Star,* p. 20.

de Groot, A. D. (1981). "Memorandum: Chess instruction in school?" In H. Lyman (Ed.), *Chess in the classroom: An answer to NIE* (pp. 1–10). Saugus, MA: Massachusetts Chess Association and American Chess Foundation. Ordering information from http://www.uschess.org/ scholastic/sc-research.html retrieved June 23, 2005: One copy of this 57-page document is five cents a page from US Chess, PO Box 3967, Crossville, TN 38557.

Evans, L. (2000, July). Larry Evans on chess. *Chess Life, 55* (7), 12–13.

Franklin, D. (1997, December). Playing games. *Hippocrates,* pp. 67–71.

Gobet, F. (1999). The father of chess psychology. *New in Chess, 8,* 84–91.

Hucks, K. (1999, June 3). Chess is catching on among the young. *The [Tacoma, WA] News Tribune*, pp. B1, B6.

Kaufman, L. (2001). Teaching chess with handicaps. *Chess Life, 56* (1), 40–41.

Kiewra, K. A., & Igo, B. (2001, December). *Distractions in the tournament rooms: Is anyone paying attention?* Paper presented at the George Koltanowski Memorial Conference on Chess and Education, Dallas, TX. Manuscript available from Dr. Kenneth A. Kiewra, kkierwra @unlserve.unl.edu.

Killigrew, B. (2000a). Profiles in chess: Bruce Pandolfini—an American master, part II. *Chess Life, 55* (6), 30–33. (Killigrew can be contacted through his Web site, http://www.briankilligrew.com)

Killigrew, B. (2000b). Profiles in chess: Bruce Pandolfini—an American master, part III. *Chess Life, 55* (7), 38–39. (Killigrew can be contacted through his Web site, http://www.briankilligrew.com.)

Krogius, N. V., & Gershunski, B. S. (1987). The world of youth hobbies: Chess (B. Pandolfini, Trans.). *Soviet Pedagogics Magazine.* Ordering information from http://www.uschess.org/scholastic/sc-research. html, retrieved June 23, 2005: One copy of this nine-page document is five cents a page from US Chess, PO Box 3967, Crossville, TN 38557.

Lawrence, A. (1993, October 22). *Female membership in USCF.* Available from US Chess, PO Box 3967, Crossville, TN 38557.

Lieberman, M. (2000). Outreach Committee. *2000 Delegates Call.* New Windsor, New York: USCF. Available from US Chess, PO Box 3967, Crossville, TN 38557.

Llada, D. (2001, January 10). Interview with Vishy Anand. *The Week In Chess Magazine.* Retrieved June 22, 2005, from http:// www.chesscenter.com/twic/event/wijk2001/anand.html.

Levy, W. (1986). *Utilizing chess to promote self-esteem in perceptually impaired students.* A teacher's guide written under the New Jersey Governor's Teacher Grant Program. Ordering information from http:// www.uschess.org/scholastic/sc-research.html, retrieved June 23, 2005. One copy of this 93 page document is available for five cents a page from US Chess, PO Box 3967, Crossville, TN 38557.

Margulies, S. (1996). *The effect of chess on reading scores*. New York: Chess-in-the-Schools. Ordering information from http://www.uschess.org/scholastic/sc-research.html, retrieved June 23, 2005: One copy of this 16-page document is available for free from U.S. Chess, PO Box 3967, Crossville, TN 38557.

McCafferty, D. (1999, June 25–27). All the right moves. *USA Weekend* newspaper supplement, pp. 6–7.

Musicant, R. (2001, September). The problem with trophies. *Chess Life, 56* (8), 54.

Parr, L. (2005). *The world chess championship and champions: 1747–2001*. Retrieved June 23, 2005 from http://www.worldchessnetwork.com/English/chessHistory/chessHistory.php.

Ramirez, M. (1992, July 5). Chess blitz a comeback hard to calculate. *The Seattle Times/Seattle Post-Intelligencer,* Pacific section, pp. 12–19.

Root, A. (1999, March/April). Safety considerations for a young child's first chess tournament. *Texas Knights*.

Root, A. (2001, spring). Queening a pawn. *Math Reader, 3* (3), pp. 4–5. Texas MathWorks, http://mathworks.txstate.edu/index.htm, is the Web site for ordering back issues of *Math Reader* and *Math Explorer.*

Root, A. (2001, December). *Chess crying: Children's preparation and tournament structure*. Paper presented at the George Koltanowski Memorial Conference on Chess and Education, Dallas, TX. Manuscript available from Dr. Alexey Root, aroot@utdallas.edu.

Silman, J. (2002). *Harry Potter: The complete position*. Retrieved June 23, 2005, from http://www.jeremysilman.com/movies_tv_js/harry_potter.html.

Storey, K. (2001, December). Retention of scholastic players: Do we need internal motivation, trophies, or reinforcement? *Chess Life, 56* (11), 52.

Tarrant, D. (2000, August 20). Making his move. *Dallas Morning News,* pp. 1F, 6F, 7F.

Thomas, K. (1999, February 26). Pleasant Valley club produces a room full of champions. *The Oregonian*, p. C3.

Tucker, C. L. (1978, December 25). She'll put you in check, mate. *Tacoma News Tribune*, sec. F.

Whalen, J., & Begley, S. (2005, March 30). In England, girls are closing gap with boys in math. *Wall Street Journal*, pp. A1, A6.

Wilgoren, J. (2005, May 17). Chess makes move to keep girls in game. *New York Times*. Retrieved June 22, 2005, from http://www.indystar.com/apps/pbcs.dll/article?AID=2005505170401.

Wojcio, M. D. (1990). The importance of chess in the classroom. *Atlantic Chess News*. Ordering information from http://www.uschess.org/scholastic/sc-research.html, retrieved June 23, 2005. One copy of this three-page document is complimentary from US Chess, PO Box 3967, Crossville, TN 38557.

Zorn, E. (1997, May 27). Having 2 kings of chess may be boon to women. *Chicago Tribune,* p. 2C1.

Dissertations

Gilbert, L. C. (1989). *Chessplayers: Gender expectations and self-fulfilling prophecy.* Unpublished doctoral dissertation, California School of Professional Psychology, Los Angeles, CA.

Root, A. W. (1999). *Instructional discourse and learning opportunities in three advanced placement United States history classrooms.* Unpublished doctoral dissertation, University of California, Los Angeles.

Video

Linton Productions (Producer). (1995). *Multiple intelligences: Developing intelligence for greater achievement* [Video recording]. Salt Lake City, Utah: Video Journal of Education 2 videocassettes (69 min.): sd., col.; 1/2 in. + 1 guidebook (12 p.) + 1 sound cassette. Series: Video Journal of Education, Vol. 4, no. 7.

Index

Academic goals, 5
Affective development, 54–55
Aging, and efficiency of players, 57
Alabama, state education standards, 86
Alaska, state education standards, 86
Alex and the Wednesday Chess Club (Wong), 39
Amazing Adventure of Dan the Pawn, The
    (Garrow), 38
American Chess Foundation ratings, 21, 111
American Chess School, 110
America's Foundation for Chess, 110
Arizona, state education standards, 87
Arkansas, state education standards, 86
Art, in chess, 20

Battleship chess, 81–83
Berkeley Chess School, 110
Bingo chessboard, 74–75
Bishop (chess piece)
    knight, compared to, 80
    legal moves, 70, 80
    point values, 70, 73, 79
Blind players, 25
Bobby Fischer Teaches Chess (Fischer and
    Mosenfelder), 110. *See also* Fischer, Bobby
Bodily kinesthetic intelligence, 50–51

    in chess charades, 77
Business, application of chess strategies in,
    56–57

Calibration, 27–28
California, state education standards, 87
*Case of the Captured Queen, The: Nancy Drew
    #147* (Keene), 38
Castled king's position, 48
Champions. *See* Grandmaster; World chess
    champions
Checkmate, 66–67
    two-rook, 64–65, 99
Checkmate at Chess City (Harper), 38
Chess camps, 112–113
Chess diagram. *See* Diagramming the
    chessboard
Chess Dream in the Garden (Sutcliff), 39
Chess for Children (Nottingham and Lawrence),
    110
Chess for Success, 110
Chess-in-the-Schools, 110
Chess Mates Foundation, 111
Chess Poems (Kusen), 38
Chess set, pieces in, 32
Children's chess books, 110

Clabbernappers (Bailey), 38
Cognitive development, 53–54
Colorado, state education standards, 87
Competition
    child's emotional status, 14–17
    of individual events, 13–14
    physical preparation, 18–19
    review of game, 17–18
Computer chess programs, in special education, 25–26
Computer That Said Steal Me, The (Levy), 38
Connecticut, state education standards, 87
Countess Veronica (Robinson), 39
Creativity, 19
Cultural literacy history teaching, 44
Curriculum
    in chess, arguments for, 2
    orientations, 4–6
    self-directed, 53–56

Deaf players, 25
Decision process in chess, 42–43
Delaware, state education standards, 87
Demonstration board, 32
Diagramming the chess board, 33–34
Differently abled players, 25–26
District of Columbia, education standards, 87

Education foundations, 110–111
Education World Site, 85
Effectiveness studies, 111
Ego development, 56
Etiquette, 67–69
Expertise, and skills set, 47–49

File, on chessboard, 64, 74
Fischer, Bobby, 25, 110
Florida state education standards, 88
    classification of animals, 75–76
Flow experience, 7–11
Free Internet Chess Server, 111

Gender gap, in competitive chess, 22–24
Georgia, state education standards, 88
Gifted players, 21–22. *See also* Prodigy players
Google usenet newsgroups, 111
Grandmaster, 24
de Groot, Adriaan D.
    chess player experiments, 41–42

optimal chess curricula, 2
transferability of chess skills, 43–44

Harry Potter and the Sorcerer's Stone (Rowling), 35–37
Hawaii, state education standards, 88
Humanistic goals, 5–6

Idaho, state education standards, 88
Illinois, state education standards, 88
Indiana, state education standards, 88
Internet Chess Club, 111
Interpersonal intelligence, 77
Iowa, state education standards, 88

Josie Gambit, The (Shura), 39
Joy Luck Club, The (Tan), 39

Kansas, state education standards, 88
Kasparov Chess Foundation, 111
Kentucky, state education standards, 89
Kids' Book of Chess (Kidder), 110
King (chess piece)
    bishop, compared to, 80
    castled, 48
    knight's tour lesson plan, 62
    legal moves, 68, 70, 80
    and pawn endgames, 80–81
    point values, 70, 73, 79
    smothered mate game, 58–59
    worksheet, 98
King's Chessboard, The (Birch), 38
Kiss of the Mermaid (Step into Reading, Step 3, paper) (Farber), 38
Knight, 70, 97

League plays, gender segregated, 58
Legal moves. *See under individual chess pieces*
Legal's mate, 72–73
Lesson plans
    battleship chess, 81–83
    charades, 77
    checkmate and stalemate, 65–67
    chessboard bingo, 74–75
    classification activities, 75–76
    etiquette, 67–69
    king and pawn dance, 80–81
    knight's tour, 62–63
    legal moves, 69–70

mathematical problem-solving, 77–79
mobility, 79–80
point values, 70, 73–74
square of the pawn, 67–69
trading card game, 70–71
two-rook checkmate, 64–65
Library chess programs, 39–40
Literature, as pedagogical tool
    Harry Potter and the Sorcerer's Stone
        (Rowling), 35–37
    Through the Looking-Glass (Carroll), 31–35
    titles, other, 38–39
Locus of control, 30–31
Louisiana, state education standards, 89

Maine, state education standards, 89
Maryland, state education standards, 89
Massachusetts, state education standards, 89
Mathematics
    problem-solving heuristics, 43, 78
    TEKS objectives, 62, 72, 74, 86
Michigan, state education standards, 89
Mind's eye, 48–49
Minnesota, state education standards, 90
Mississippi, state education standards, 90
Missouri, state education standards, 90
Mobility, 79–80
Montana, state education standards, 90
Moral development, 29–30
Moreno, Fernando, 54
Mort the Sport (Kraus), 38
Multiple intelligences theory, 5, 47. *See also*
    Bodily kinesthetic intelligence; Spatial
    intelligence
My System (Nimzowitsch), 110

National Scholastic Chess Foundation, 111
Nebraska, state education standards, 90
Nevada, state education standards, 91
New Hampshire, state education standards, 90
New history dialogic teaching, 45
New Jersey, state education standards, 91
New Mexico, state education standards, 91
New York, state education standards, 91
Nonprofit sponsors, 110–111
North Carolina, state education standards, 90
North Dakota, state education standards, 90
Notation
    algebraic, 35, 96

descriptive, 35
in scholastic chess tournaments, 14–15
score sheet, 17, 18
technique, 63

Odds system of pairing players, 26–27
Ohio, state education standards, 91
Oklahoma, state education standards, 92
*1001 Winning Chess Sacrifices and
    Combinations* (Reinfeld), 110
Oregon, state education standards, 92

Pairing systems, 26–28
Pandolfini, Bruce, 56–57
Passed pawn, 83
Pattern recognition, 48
Pawn (chess piece)
    chain, 48
    and king endgames, 80–81
    legal moves, 68, 70, 80
    passed, 83
    point values, 70, 73, 79
    promotion, 67, 68
    queening, 31–34
    square of, 68
Pawn Power in Chess (Kmoch), 110
Pennsylvania, state education standards, 92
Physical fitness, 18–19
Piagetian approach to teaching, 45
Point values, 70
    checkmate and stalemate, 66
Politics of chess, 111
Postmortem, 18
Practical Chess Endings (Keres), 110
Problem-solving heuristic, 42–43
Prodigy players, 25. *See also* Gifted players

Queen (chess piece), 70, 73, 79–80
Queening the pawn, 31–34

Ranks, on chessboard, 64
Rating system. *See* American Chess Foundation
    ratings
Reading objectives of TEKS, 32, 36, 50, 72, 86
    and comprehension, 49–50
Rhode Island, state education standards, 92
Rook (chess piece)
    checkmate with two pieces, 64–65, 99
    legal moves, 70, 80

point values, 70, 73, 79
Root, Doug, 110
Round robin tournament, 27
Rules of chess
  beginning moves, 78
  castled king's position, 48
  checkmate and stalemate, 66–67, 81
  legal moves (*see individual pieces*)
  opposition, 81
  pawn chains, 48
  queening the pawn, 34
  resources, 109–110
  smothered mate game, 58–59
  starting position, 56
  touch move, 51
  two-rook checkmate, 64–65
Runner's high, in chess players, 7–8

Satisfaction, from flow experience, 8
Savants, 25
Scholar's mate, 72
Scholastic chess tournaments, 15–16
Searching for Bobby Fischer (Waitzkin), 39
Self-actualization, 8
Self-directed curriculum, 53–56
Senior chess players, 57
Smothered mate game, 58–59
Social adaptationist curriculum, 4
Social reconstructionist curriculum, 4
Social skills development, 55
Software products in teaching, 109, 110
South Carolina, state education standards, 92
South Dakota, state education standards, 92
Southern California Chess Federation Women's
  Chess League, 58
Spatial ability and gender gap, 22–23
Spatial intelligence, 49–50
Special education students, 25–26
Stalemate, 66–67
  with king and pawn, 81
Stand Tall, Harry (Mahony), 39
State Affiliates Directory for chess, 111
State standards. *See individual states*
Success Chess Schools, 111
SuperNationalsII, 14–15

Susan Polgar National Invitational for Girls, 24
Swiss system of pairing players, 27–28
Systemic curriculum, 4–5

Teaching methods, 44–45
Tennessee, state education standards, 92
Texas Essential Knowledge Skills, 1–2, 93
  mathematics objectives, 62, 72, 74, 86
  problem-solving heuristics, 43
  state reading objectives, 32, 36, 50, 72, 86
Think Like a King School Chess Software
  System, 110
Through the Looking-Glass (Carroll), 31–35
Touch move rule, 51
Tournament directors, behavior in scholastic
  chess, 15
Tournament rounds. *See also* League plays;
  Pairing systems
  gender-segregated, 24–25
  notation in, 14–15
  round robin, 27
  rules, 14
  scholastic tournaments, 15–16
Trading card game, 70–71
Trophy rewards in youth sports, 16
Two-rook checkmate, 64–65

United States Chess Federation, 16, 111
U.S. Championship, 24
U.S. Women's Championship, 24
Utah, state education standards, 93
UT TeleCampus, chess course, 2–3

Vampire State Building (Levy), 38
Vermont, state education standards, 93
Virginia, state education standards, 93
Visual information, 48–49

Washington, state education standards, 93
Web resources, 111–112
Weeramantry, Sunil, 44
West Virginia, state education standards, 93
Wisconsin, state education standards, 93
World chess champions, 21–22
Wyoming, state education standards, 93

ABOUT THE AUTHOR

DR. ALEXEY ROOT has a PhD in education from UCLA. Her work history includes full-time public high school teaching (social studies and English) and substitute teaching at all grade levels. Root has been a tournament chess player since she was nine years old. Her most notable chess accomplishment was winning the U.S. Women's championship in 1989. For the last six years, Root has been a senior lecturer at the University of Texas at Dallas (UTD). She has taught UTD education classes, tutored prospective teachers for certification exams, and supervised student teachers. Root's current assignment for UTD is to teach online education courses that explore the uses of chess in classrooms. Root also teaches chess at her children's schools and at summer chess camps. She lives in Denton, TX, with her husband, Doug; her children, Clarissa and William; and two house rabbits. Dr. Root's e-mail is alexey.root@gmail.com.